THINGS

MONEY

CAN'T BUY™

Dr. Robert Mukes

FAITH FOOD
™
THE LIVING BREAD

All scripture references, unless otherwise indicated, are taken from the King James Version (KJV) of the Holy Bible.

Other Version:
New International Version (NIV)
Amplified Version (AMP)

Things Money Can't Buy™
Is a trademark of Dr. Robert Mukes

Wisdom of Wealth™
Is a trademark of Dr. Robert Mukes

Library of Congress Control Number: 2010908020

Copyright © 2004 by Dr. Robert Mukes
First Printing 2005
Second Printing 2025

ISBN 978-0-9701799-4-4

Published, printed and distributed in Southaven, Mississippi, in the United States of America by Faith Food, LLC.

Cover and logos design by Robert Mukes

DEDICATION

This book is dedicated to all who desire
the truth. The word of God teaches you that
Jesus has already paid the price in full for
everything that pertains to life and godliness.

Contents

INTRODUCTION

David said this of the word of God

"The words of the Lord are pure words, as silver tried in a furnace of the earth, purified seven times." *(Ps. 12:6)*

The number seven stands for completion and perfection. The word of God is the only thing that is complete. The word will teach you that riches are not an end to life. They are only a means in assisting you in experiencing God's expected plans for your life (Jer. 29:11;Eccl.10:19,7:12-14) and also, for you to be a good Samaritan to those that are in need (1 Tim. 6:17-19; 1 John 3:17). Sadly, the enemy has tricked many in thinking that the kingdom of riches - means completeness. Be-ware of the works of the enemy. Money is a temporal thing (Prov. 27:24; 2 Cor. 4:18). The word of God teaches you that it is in Him (God) you live, move and have your being (Acts 17:28-30). Your completeness is your new life hidden with Christ in God (Col. 3:1-3; 2 Cor. 3:5,9:8).

The words of Paul to the Colossians

"As ye have therefore received Christ Jesus the Lord, so walk ye in him. [10] And ye are complete in him, which is the head of all principality and power." *(Col. 2:6,10)*

Riches are to be used for the furthering of God's kingdom work. This kingdom work is simply the saving and transformation of souls to the glory of God.

God wants you to have the right perspective on money. Whatever material blessings He places in your stewardship, they are to be used to glorify Him in a holy manner.

"As every man hath received the gift, even so minister the same one to another, as good stewards of the manifold grace of God. [11] If any man speak, let him speak as the oracles of God; if any man minister, let him do it as of the ability which God giveth: that God in all things may be glorified through Jesus Christ, to whom be praise and dominion for ever and ever. Amen." *(1 Pet. 4:10-11)*

I will continue by highlighting a few truths concerning the true ownership of all things.

Truth #1
God can't lie

"God is not a man, that he should lie; neither the son of man, that he should repent: hath he said, and shall he not do it? or hath he spoken, and shall he not make it good." *(Num. 23:19)*

"That by two immutable things, in which it was impossible for God to lie, we might have a strong consolation, who have fled for refuge to lay hold upon the hope set before us." *(Heb. 6:18)*

Truth #2
Everything belongs to God and was created for His pleasure

"Thou art worthy, O Lord, to receive glory and honour and power: for thou hast created all things, and for thy pleasure they are and were created." *(Rev. 4:11)*

As spoken by David

"The earth is the Lord's, and the fulness thereof; the world, and they that dwell therein." *(Ps. 24:1)*

Re-spoken by Paul

"For the earth is the Lord's, and the fullness thereof." *(1 Cor. 10:26)*

God owns the silver and gold

"The silver is mine, and the gold is mine, saith the LORD of hosts." *(Hag. 2:8)* See also. Gen. 2:11-12; Lev. 27:30; Josh. 6:19; Mal. 3:8; Joel 3:5

THINGS MONEY CAN'T BUY

God owns all the land

"The land shall not be sold for ever: for the land is mine; for ye are strangers and sojourners with me." *(Lev. 25:23)*   Early church. Acts 4:32,34,35

God owns all the livestock

"For every beast of the forest is mine, and the cattle upon a thousand hills." *(Ps. 50:10)*

God owns and controls all things (Ps. 103:19)

"Thine, O Lord, is the greatness, and the power, and the glory, and the victory, and the majesty: for all that is in the heaven and in the earth is thine; thine is the kingdom, O Lord, and thou art exalted as head above all. Both riches and honour come of thee, and thou reignest over all; and in thine hand is power and might; and in thine hand it is to make great, and to give strength unto all." *(1 Chr. 29:11-12)*   See also. 2 Chr. 20:5-6; Gen. 14:19

"For by him were all things created, that are in heaven, and that are in earth, visible and invisible, whether they be thrones, or dominions, or principalities, or powers: all things were created by him, and for him: And he is before all things, and by him all things consist." *(Col. 1:16-17)*

"For of him, and through him, and to him, are all things: to whom be glory for ever. Amen." *(Rom. 11:36)*

"Behold, the heaven and the heaven of heavens is the Lord's thy God, the earth also, with all that therein is." *(Deut. 10:14)* See also. Job 41:11

God even owns you

"For ye are bought with a price: therefore glorify God in your body, and in your spirit, which are God's."*(1 Cor. 6:20)* (Ps. 24:1; Ezek. 18:4; Rom. 14:8)

"Who gave himself for our sins, that he might deliver us from this present evil world, according to the will of God and our Father." *(Gal. 1:4)* John 1:3

"What? know ye not that your body is the temple of the Holy Ghost which is in you, which ye have of God, and ye are not your own." *(1 Cor. 6:19)*

Truth #3
One of God's blessings – wealth

"The blessing of the LORD, it maketh rich, and he added no sorrow with it." *(Prov. 10:22)*

Truth #4
You are better off with a little and God, than a lot without Him

"Better is the poor that walketh in his uprightness, than he that is perverse in his ways, though he be rich." *(Prov. 28:6)*

Truth #5
A person not knowing their own heart

"He who trusts in himself is a fool, but he who walks in wisdom is kept safe." *(Prov. 28:26 NIV)*

"The heart is deceitful above all things, and desperately wicked: who can know it." *(Jer. 17:9)* See also. Jer. 17:7

Truth #6
The wrong perception of many financially blessed persons

"And thou say in thine heart, My power and the might of mine hand hath gotten me this wealth." *(Deut. 8:17)*

You are to be reminded that it is a blessing from God

"But if thou shalt remember the LORD thy God: for it is he that giveth thee power to get wealth, that he may establish his covenant which he sware unto thy fathers, as it is this day. And it shall be, if thou do at all forget the LORD thy God, and walk after other gods, and serve them, and worship them, I testify against you this day that ye shall surely perish." *(Deut. 8:18-19)*

"Then he answered and spake unto me, saying, This is the word of the LORD unto Zerubbabel, saying, Not by might, nor by power, but by my spirit, saith the LORD of hosts." *(Zech. 4:6)*

God even blesses the wicked - that they might come to repentance

"Or despiset thou the riches of his goodness and forebearence and longsuffering; not knowing that the goodness of God leadeth thee to repentance." *(Rom. 2:4)*

Truth #7
Put God first in your life

"For after all these things do the Gentiles seek: for your heavenly Father knoweth that ye have need of all these things." *(Matt. 6:32)*

"But seek ye first the kingdom of God, and his righteousness; and all these things shall be added unto you." (*Matt. 6:33)*

Truth #8
Two kinds of people

"A good man out of the good treasure of the heart bringeth forth good things: and an evil man out of the evil treasure bringeth forth evil things." *(Matt. 12:35)*

Truth #9
Nothing is greater than salvation

"For what is a man profited, if he shall gain the whole world, and lose his own soul? Or what shall a man give in exchange for his soul." *(Matt. 16:26)*

Truth #10
The source of life

"For in him (God) we live, and move, and have our being; as certain also of your own poets have said, For we are also his offspring." *(Acts 17:28)*

"The thief (devil) cometh not, but for to steal, and to kill, and to destroy: I (Jesus) am come that they might have life, and that they might have it more abundantly." *(John 10:10)*

Truth #11
Don't lose focus

"Trust not in oppression, and become not vain in robbery: if riches increase, set not your heart upon them." *(Ps. 62:10)* See also. 1 Tim. 6:17

Truth #12
Avoid the spirit of covetousness and greed

"If I have put my trust in gold or said to pure gold, 'You are my security,' if I have rejoiced over my great wealth, the fortune my hands had gained, if I have regarded the sun in its radiance or the moon moving in splendor, so that my heart was secretly enticed and my hand offered them a kiss of homage, then these also would be sins to be judged, for I would have been unfaithful to God on high." *(Job 31:24-28 NIV)*

"And he said unto them, Take heed, and beware of covetousness: for a man's life consisteth not in the abundance of the things which he posseth." *(Luke 12:15)*

Truth #13
Death to those living after the flesh

"But put ye own the Lord Jesus Christ, and make no provision for the flesh, to fulfil the lusts thereof." *(Rom. 13:14)*

"For if ye live after the flesh, ye shall die." *(Rom. 8:13 Part A)*

The sinful pleasures of money are only good for a season (for the occasion only, a while, temporal or temporary)

"By faith Moses, when he was come to years, refused to be called the son of Pharaoh's daughter; Choosing rather to suffer affliction with the people of God, than to enjoy the pleasures of sin for a season."
(Heb. 11:24-25)

Truth #14
Life to those living after the Spirit

"Therefore, brethren, we are debtors, not to the flesh, to live after the flesh. But if ye through the Spirit do mortify the deeds of the body, ye shall live."
(Rom. 8:12 Verse 13, Part A)

"I am crucified with Christ: nevertheless I live; yet not I, but Christ liveth in me: and the life which I now live in the flesh I live by the faith of the Son of God, who loved me, and gave himself for me." *(Gal. 2:20)*

Truth #15
God's mercy is everlasting

"For the LORD is good; his mercy is everlasting; and his truth endureth to all generations." *(Ps. 100:5)*

In order to be a faithful financial steward with the finances of God, you must learn to wisely invest in the temporal things here on earth (Matt. 24:35; 2 Pet. 3:10 - See "The Investment Process", from my books - "What To Do With Money™ & The Need Meeter™). However, when you invest in the spiritual things, they will last forever, and you will be found faithful and richly rewarded. *(Matt. 6:19-21)*

CHAPTER 1

SALVATION (restoration of your relationship with God)

"They that trust in their wealth, and boast themselves in the multitude of their riches; None of them can by any means redeem his brother, nor give to God a ransom for Him." *(Ps. 49:6-7)*

"Neither is there salvation in any other: for there is none other name under heaven given among men, whereby we must be saved." *(Acts 4:12)*

This none other name includes all names beside Jesus. They are names such as: money; family; denomination; doctrines of men; creeds; religions; idols; education; law; works; social status or any other name.

"For what shall it profit a man, if he shall gain the whole world, and lose his own soul." *(Mark 8:36)*

"For God so loved the world, that he gave his only begotten Son, that whosoever believeth in him should not perish, but have everlasting life." *(John 3:16)*   See also Rev. 22:17

How you are not redeemed

"(For the redemption of their soul is precious, and it ceaseth for ever:) [9] That he should still live for ever, and not see corruption." *(Ps. 49:8-9)*

"Forasmuch as ye know that ye were not redeemed with corruptible things, as silver and gold, from your vain conversation received by tradition from your fathers." *(1 Pet. 1:18)*

"For thus saith the Lord, Ye have sold yourselves for nought; and ye shall be redeemed without money." *(Is. 52:3)*

"Ho, every one that thirsteth, come ye to the waters, and he that hath no money; come ye, buy, and eat; yea, come, buy wine and milk without money and without price." *(Is. 55:1)*

"Surely he (man) will have no respite from his craving; he cannot save himself by his treasure." *(Job 20:20 NIV)*   See also. Job 27:8; Ps. 118:14

"Neither their silver nor their gold shall be able to deliver them in the day of the Lord's wrath; but the whole land shall be devoured by the fire of his jealousy: for he shall make even a speedy riddance of all them that dwell in the land." *(Zeph. 1:18)*

Water baptism is the acknowledgement of a good conscience toward God. (1 Pet. 3:21 AMP).

How you are redeemed

Blood of Jesus

"But with the precious blood of Christ, as of a lamb without blemish and without spot: Who verily was foreordained before the foundation of the world, but was manifest in these last times for you, Who by him do believe in God, that raised him up from the dead, and gave him glory; that your faith and hope might be in God." *(1 Pet. 1:19-21)*

See also. Rom. 5:10-11; Rev. 1:5

"And from Jesus Christ, who is the faithful witness, and the first begotten of the dead, and the prince of the kings of the earth. Unto him that loved us, and washed us from our sins in his own blood." *(Rev. 1:5)*

"Being born again, not of corruptible seed, but of incorruptible, by the word of God, which liveth and abideth for ever." *(1 Pet. 1:23)*

  It is only by the power of the blood that true atonement of the soul can take place (Leviticus 17:11; Matthew 26:28; Hebrews 9:11-28, 10:1-23; 1 John 1:7).

By grace (God's unmerited favor) and faith (trusting and believing God's word) through Jesus Christ

"For by grace are ye saved through faith; and that not of yourselves: it is the gift of God: Not of works, lest any man should boast." *(Eph. 2:8-9)*

THINGS MONEY CAN'T BUY

For those who desire to experience salvation

"For all have sinned, and come short of the glory of God." *(Rom. 3:23)*

"For the wages of sin is death; but the gift of God is eternal life through Jesus Christ our Lord." *(Rom. 6:23)*

"But God commendeth his love toward us, in that, while we were yet sinners, Christ died for us." *(Rom. 5:8)*

Repent (Rom. 10:17; Ezek. 18:30-32; Mark 2:17; Acts 3:19; 2 Pet. 3:9).

"That if thou shalt confess with thy mouth the Lord Jesus, and shalt believe in thine heart that God hath raised him from the dead, thou shalt be saved." *(Rom. 10:9)*

The story of a poor man and a rich man final resting place

"There was a certain rich man, which was clothed in purple and fine linen, and fared sumptuously every day: [20] And there was a certain beggar named Lazarus, which was laid at his gate, full of sores, [21] And desiring to be fed with the crumbs which fell from the rich man's table: moreover the dogs came and licked his sores. [22] And it came to pass, that the beggar died, and was carried by the angels into Abraham's bosom: the rich man also died, and was buried; [23] And in hell he lift up his eyes, being in torments, and seeth Abraham afar off, and Lazarus in his bosom. [24] And he cried and said, Father Abraham, have mercy on me, and send Lazarus, that he may dip the tip of his finger in water, and cool my tongue; for I am tormented in this flame. [25] But Abraham said, Son, remember that thou in thy lifetime receivedst thy good things, and likewise Lazarus evil things: but now he is comforted, and thou art tormented. [26] And beside all this, between us and you there is a great gulf fixed: so that they which would pass from hence to you cannot; neither can they pass to us, that would come from thence. [27] Then he said, I pray thee therefore, father, that thou wouldest send him to my father's house: [28] For I have five brethren; that he may testify unto them, lest they also come into this place of torment. [29] Abraham saith unto him, They have Moses and the prophets; let them hear them. [30] And he said, Nay, father Abraham: but if one went unto them from the dead, they will repent. [31] And he said unto him, If they hear not Moses and the prophets, neither will they be persuaded, though one rose from the dead." *(Luke 16:19-31)*

CHAPTER 2

ETERNAL LIFE (life with God - without end)

The story of the rich young ruler

"And, behold, one came and said unto him, Good Master, what good thing shall I do, that I may have eternal life? [17] And he said unto him, Why callest thou me good? there is none good but one, that is, God: but if thou wilt enter into life, keep the commandments. [18] He saith unto him, Which? Jesus said, Thou shalt do no murder, Thou shalt not commit adultery, Thou shalt not steal, Thou shalt not bear false witness,[19] Honour thy father and thy mother: and, Thou shalt love thy neighbour as thyself. [20] The young man saith unto him, All these things have I kept from my youth up: what lack I yet? [21] Jesus said unto him, If thou wilt be perfect, go and sell that thou hast, and give to the poor, and thou shalt have treasure in heaven: and come and follow me. [22] But when the young man heard that saying, he went away sorrowful: for he had great possessions. [23] Then said Jesus unto his disciples, Verily I say unto you, That a rich man shall hardly enter into the kingdom of heaven. [24] And again I say unto you, It is easier for a camel to go through the eye of a needle, than for a rich man to enter into the kingdom of God. [25] When his disciples heard it, they were exceedingly amazed, saying, Who then can be saved? [26] But Jesus beheld them, and said unto them, With men this is impossible; but with God all things are possible." *(Matt. 19:16-26)*

Jesus said that it is very difficult for a rich person, although not impossible, to inherit eternal life. He instructed the rich man to do three things.

1. Sale all your goods. Jesus was saying to him, get deliverance from all earthly things - renounce the love of the world. You must begin to walk in the Spirit by setting your mind on things above, that you might inherit eternal life. See additional references. Col. 3:1-3; Gal. 5:16; 1 John 5:11-12

2. Give to the poor. Ps. 41:1-2; Prov. 28:27

3. Follow me. Follow comes from the Greek word Akoloutheo "Ak-ol-oo-theh-o". It is present tense. It means to be in union with – to be in the same way with – to accompany (as a disciple) that you might reach a final destination.

Jesus wanted the rich man to be delivered from the idol god of money.

See the story of the rich man Zacchaeus whom Jesus saved. Luke 19:1-10.

"Is any thing too hard for the Lord? At the time appointed I will return unto thee, according to the time of life, and Sarah shall have a son."
(Gen 18:14)

God blessed Abraham's wife Sara with a son when she was ninety years old.

Job said this of God:

"I know that thou canst do every thing, and that no thought can be withholden from thee." *(Job 42:2)*

"They that trust in the Lord shall be as mount Zion, which cannot be removed, but abideth for ever. [2] As the mountains are round about Jerusalem, so the Lord is round about his people from henceforth even for ever. [3] For the rod of the wicked shall not rest upon the lot of the righteous; lest the righteous put forth their hands unto iniquity. [4] Do good, O Lord, unto those that be good, and to them that are upright in their hearts. [5] As for such as turn aside unto their crooked ways, the Lord shall lead them forth with the workers of iniquity: but peace shall be upon Israel."
(Ps. 125:1-5)

"And as it is appointed unto men once to die, but after this the judgment."
(Heb. 9:27)

What will be your verdict ? If guilty, your eternal home will be destruction in the lake of fire.

THINGS MONEY CAN'T BUY

The abiding law

To experience eternal life with God, you must maintain your spiritual relationship and fellowship with God.

"Receiving the end of your faith, even the salvation of your souls."
(1 Pet. 1:9)

The word abideth comes from the Greek word Meno #3306 Strong's. It means to (continue – dwell – endure – be present – remain).

"Whosoever transgresseth, and abideth not in the doctrine of Christ, hath not God. He that abideth in the doctrine of Christ, he hath both the Father and the Son." *(2 John 1:9)*

"Looking unto Jesus the author and finisher of our faith; who for the joy that was set before him endured the cross, despising the shame, and is set down at the right hand of the throne of God." *(Heb. 12:2)*

"For God so loved the world, that he gave his only begotten Son, that whosoever believeth in him should not perish, but have everlasting life. [17] For God sent not his Son into the world to condemn the world; but that the world through him might be saved. [18] He that believeth on him is not condemned: but he that believeth not is condemned already, because he hath not believed in the name of the only begotten Son of God. [19] And this is the condemnation, that light is come into the world, and men loved darkness rather than light, because their deeds were evil. [20] For every one that doeth evil hateth the light, neither cometh to the light, lest his deeds should be reproved." *(John 3:16-20)*

The word 'Believe'. Present tense (faith - commit - continual trust in God).

"And this is the record, that God hath given to us eternal life, and this life is in his Son. [12] He that hath the Son hath life; and he that hath not the Son of God hath not life. [13] These things have I written unto you that believe on the name of the Son of God; that ye may know that ye have eternal life, and that ye may believe on the name of the Son of God." *(1 John 5:11-13)*
See also. John 11:25-26

The question then is. Can you willingly stop abiding in Jesus ?

Let us look at a backslidden church (Laodicea).

"And unto the angel of the church of the Laodiceans write; These things saith the Amen, the faithful and true witness, the beginning of the creation of God; [15] I know thy works, that thou art neither cold nor hot: I would thou wert cold or hot. [16] So then because thou art lukewarm, and neither cold nor hot, I will spue thee out of my mouth. [17] Because thou sayest, I am rich, and increased with goods, and have need of nothing; and knowest not that thou art wretched, and miserable, and poor, and blind, and naked: [18] I counsel thee to buy of me gold tried in the fire, that thou mayest be rich; and white raiment, that thou mayest be clothed, and that the shame of thy nakedness do not appear; and anoint thine eyes with eyesalve, that thou mayest see. [19] As many as I love, I rebuke and chasten: be zealous therefore, and repent. [20] Behold, I stand at the door, and knock: if any man hear my voice, and open the door, I will come in to him, and will sup with him, and he with me. [21] To him that overcometh will I grant to sit with me in my throne, even as I also overcame, and am set down with my Father in his throne. [22] He that hath an ear, let him hear what the Spirit saith unto the churches." *(Rev. 3:14-22)*

The devil tricked them with a false vision - that there is security in riches without abiding in Christ.

"Paul, an apostle of Jesus Christ by the will of God, according to the promise of life which is in Christ Jesus." *(2 Tim. 1:1)*

"Labour not for the meat which perisheth, but for that meat which endureth unto everlasting life, which the Son of man shall give unto you: for him hath God the Father sealed." *(John 6:27)*

Eternal life is a promise for those who abide in Jesus until the end.

Your end-state in this life will determine your future.

"He that is unjust, let him be unjust still: and he which is filthy, let him be filthy still: and he that is righteous, let him be righteous still: and he that is holy, let him be holy still." *(Rev. 22:11)* See also. Ezek. 33:10-20;Rev. 22:14

Your name can be blotted out of the book of life (names of the righteous).

Moses' prayer for the children of God

"And Moses returned unto the Lord, and said, Oh, this people have sinned a great sin, and have made them gods of gold. [32] Yet now, if thou wilt forgive their sin; and if not, blot me, I pray thee, out of thy book which thou hast written. [33] And the Lord said unto Moses, Whosoever hath sinned against me, him will I blot out of my book." *(Ex. 32:31-33)*

Prophecy of David concerning Judas and those who crucified Christ

"Let their table become a snare before them: and that which should have been for their welfare, let it become a trap. [23] Let their eyes be darkened, that they see not; and make their loins continually to shake. [24] Pour out thine indignation upon them, and let thy wrathful anger take hold of them. [25] Let their habitation be desolate; and let none dwell in their tents. [26] For they persecute him whom thou hast smitten; and they talk to the grief of those whom thou hast wounded. [27] Add iniquity unto their iniquity: and let them not come into thy righteousness. [28] Let them be blotted out of the book of the living, and not be written with the righteous." *(Ps. 69:22-28)*

"For it is written in the book of Psalms, Let his habitation be desolate, and let no man dwell therein: and his bishoprick let another take." *(Acts 1:20)*

"He that overcometh, the same shall be clothed in white raiment; and I will not blot out his name out of the book of life, but I will confess his name before my Father, and before his angels." *(Rev. 3:5)*

Let us look at a few examples of some who once had the right relationship with God - but ended up separated from God.

Judas Iscariot

Biblical proofs of his new life in Christ.

He was considered one of the great shepherd's many sheep.

"Behold, I send you forth as sheep in the midst of wolves: be ye therefore wise as serpents, and harmless as doves." *(Matt. 19:16)*

"And Jesus said unto them, Verily I say unto you, That ye which have followed me, in the regeneration when the Son of man shall sit in the throne of his glory, ye also shall sit upon twelve thrones, judging the twelve tribes of Israel." *(Matt. 19:28)*

Ordained of God to preach the gospel with power

"And he goeth up into a mountain, and calleth unto him whom he would: and they came unto him. [14] And he ordained twelve, that they should be with him, and that he might send them forth to preach, [15] And to have power to heal sicknesses, and to cast out devils." *(Mark 3:13-15)*

He once had the promise of eternal life

"As thou hast given him power over all flesh, that he should give eternal life to as many as thou hast given him." *(John 17:2)*

"While I was with them in the world, I kept them in thy name: those that thou gavest me I have kept, and none of them is lost, but the son of perdition; that the scripture might be fulfilled." *(John 17:12)*

As noted previously, he was once saved with proof of it having his name in the book of life. Ps. 69:25-28; Luke 10:20; Acts 1:20; Mark 6:13

He was part of the early apostolic church

"And in those days Peter stood up in the midst of the disciples, and said, (the number of names together were about an hundred and twenty,) [16] Men and brethren, this scripture must needs have been fulfilled, which the Holy Ghost by the mouth of David spake before concerning Judas, which was guide to them that took Jesus. [17] For he was numbered with us, and had obtained part of this ministry." *(Acts 1:15-17)*

See also. Matt. 10:1-20

Judas fell by transgression

"That he may take part of this ministry and apostleship, from which Judas by transgression fell, that he might go to his own place." *(Acts 1:25)*
See also. Mark 14:21

Part of Judas' betrayal of Jesus was money. This is one of the devil's primary weapons he uses to cause the saints to fall into the state of apostasy.

"Then one of the twelve, called Judas Iscariot, went unto the chief priests, [15] And said unto them, What will ye give me, and I will deliver him unto you? And they covenanted with him for thirty pieces of silver. [16] And from that time he sought opportunity to betray him." *(Matt. 26:14-16)*

King Saul

"So Saul died for his transgression which he committed against the Lord, even against the word of the Lord, which he kept not, and also for asking counsel of one that had a familiar spirit, to enquire of it; [14] And enquired not of the Lord: therefore he slew him, and turned the kingdom unto David the son of Jesse." *(1 Chr. 10:13-14)*

"And the soul that turneth after such as have familiar spirits, and after wizards, to go a whoring after them, I will even set my face against that soul, and will cut him off from among his people." *(Lev. 20:6)*

Achan

"Israel hath sinned, and they have also transgressed my covenant which I commanded them: for they have even taken of the accursed thing, and have also stolen, and dissembled also, and they have put it even among their own stuff. [12] Therefore the children of Israel could not stand before their enemies, but turned their backs before their enemies, because they were accursed: neither will I be with you any more, except ye destroy the accursed from among you. [13] Up, sanctify the people, and say, Sanctify yourselves against to morrow: for thus saith the Lord God of Israel, There is an accursed thing in the midst of thee, O Israel: thou canst not stand before thine enemies, until ye take away the accursed thing from among you.   [14] In the morning therefore ye shall be brought according to your tribes: and it shall be, that the tribe which the Lord taketh shall come according to the families thereof; and the family which the Lord shall take shall come by households; and the household which the Lord shall take shall come man by man. [15] And it shall be, that he that is taken with the accursed thing shall be burnt with fire, he and all that he hath: because he hath transgressed the covenant of the Lord, and because he hath wrought folly in Israel." *(Josh. 7:11-15)*

"So Joshua sent messengers, and they ran unto the tent; and, behold, it was hid in his tent, and the silver under it. [23] And they took them out of the midst of the tent, and brought them unto Joshua, and unto all the children of Israel, and laid them out before the Lord. [24] And Joshua, and all Israel with him, took Achan the son of Zerah, and the silver, and the garment, and the wedge of gold, and his sons, and his daughters, and his oxen, and his asses, and his sheep, and his tent, and all that he had: and they brought them unto the valley of Achor. [25] And Joshua said, Why hast thou troubled us? the Lord shall trouble thee this day. And all Israel stoned him with stones, and burned them with fire, after they had stoned them with stones. [26] And they raised over him a great heap of stones unto this day. So the Lord turned from the fierceness of his anger. Wherefore the name of that place was called, The valley of Achor, unto this day." *(Josh. 7:22-26)*

Many disciples of Jesus

"But there are some of you that believe not. For Jesus knew from the beginning who they were that believed not, and who should betray him. [65] And he said, Therefore said I unto you, that no man can come unto me, except it were given unto him of my Father. [66] From that time many of his disciples went back, and walked no more with him. [67] Then said Jesus unto the twelve, Will ye also go away? [68] Then Simon Peter answered him, Lord, to whom shall we go? thou hast the words of eternal life."
(John 6:64-68)

The answer to those who fall away from God is total separation from God

"For if we sin wilfully after that we have received the knowledge of the truth, there remaineth no more sacrifice for sins, [27] But a certain fearful looking for of judgment and fiery indignation, which shall devour the adversaries. [28] He that despised Moses' law died without mercy under two or three witnesses: [29] Of how much sorer punishment, suppose ye, shall he be thought worthy, who hath trodden under foot the Son of God, and hath counted the blood of the covenant, wherewith he was sanctified, an unholy thing, and hath done despite unto the Spirit of grace? [30] For we know him that hath said, Vengeance belongeth unto me, I will recompense, saith the Lord. And again, The Lord shall judge his people. [31] It is a fearful thing to fall into the hands of the living God. [32] But call to remembrance the former days, in which, after ye were illuminated, ye endured a great fight of afflictions; [33] Partly, whilst ye were made a gazingstock both by reproaches and afflictions; and partly, whilst ye became companions of them that were so used. [34] For ye had compassion of me in my bonds, and took joyfully the spoiling of your goods, knowing in yourselves that ye have in heaven a better and an enduring substance. [35] Cast not away therefore your confidence, which hath great recompence of reward. [36] For ye have need of patience, that, after ye have done the will of God, ye might receive the promise. [37] For yet a little while, and he that shall come will come, and will not tarry. [38] Now the just shall live by faith: but if any man draw back, my soul shall have no pleasure in him. [39] But we are not of them who draw back unto perdition; but of them that believe to the saving of the soul." *(Heb. 10:26-39)*

The church at Ephesus

"Nevertheless I have somewhat against thee, because thou hast left thy first love. [5] Remember therefore from whence thou art fallen, and repent, and do the first works; or else I will come unto thee quickly, and will remove thy candlestick out of his place, except thou repent." *(Rev. 2:4-5)*

If you lose your first love, you lose God

"Beloved, let us love one another: for love is of God; and every one that loveth is born of God, and knoweth God." *(1 John 4:7)*

"And I give unto them eternal life; and they shall never perish, neither shall any man pluck them out of my hand. [29] My Father, which gave them me, is greater than all; and no man is able to pluck them out of my Father's hand. [30] I and my Father are one." *(John 10:28-30)*

If this is so, then, the only way for you to be removed from the protection of His hand, is by exercising your free will and voluntarily removing yourself.

The following references show how Satan sinned and lost his secured estate with God.

(Col. 1:16; Gen 1:31; Ps. 148:2-5; Ezek. 28:11-19; Is. 14:12-15; Luke 10:18; 1 Tim. 3:6)

As you read in the previous pages, in Paul's letter to the Hebrews, he reminded them that the just shall live by faith. Heb. 10:26-39

When Christ becomes of no effect to you, you will fall from grace

"Christ is become of no effect unto you, whosoever of you are justified by the law; ye are fallen from grace." *(Gal. 5:4)*

See additional references. Chapters one, three and five of Galatians.

"For God sent not his Son into the world to condemn the world; but that the world through him might be saved. [18] He that believeth on him is not condemned: but he that believeth not is condemned already, because he hath not believed in the name of the only begotten Son of God." *(John 3:17-18)*

See additional references on eternal life. 2 Chr. 7:19-20; Jer. 12:14-17; 18:7-17; 31:28-30; 45:4; Ezek. 3:20; 17:9; 18:4,24-32; 33:12-20; Job 27:8

THINGS MONEY CAN'T BUY

The words of Jesus on salvation

"And ye shall be hated of all men for my name's sake: but he that endureth to the end shall be saved." *(Matt. 10:22)*

"And because iniquity shall abound, the love of many shall wax cold. [13] But he that shall endure unto the end, the same shall be saved." *(Matt. 24:12-13)*

A gift from God

"For the wages of sin is death; but the gift of God is eternal life through Jesus Christ our Lord." *(Rom. 6:23)* See also. Rom. 3:24,5:15-18; Eph.2:8-9; John 6:27

The key to eternal life

"And the world passeth away, and the lust thereof: **but he that doeth the will of God abideth for ever**." *(1 John 2:17)*

"The highway of the upright is to depart from evil: he that keepeth his way preserveth his soul." *(Prov. 16:17)*

The key to eternal life - is for you to do the will of the Father on a daily basis by remaining in Christ - thus overcoming in victory. See other references.   John 15:1-6; 1 John 2:24-25, 3:24; Rev. 3:2-5,12,14-22,22:18-19; Rom. 11:23 (AMP)

Warning of falling away or abandoning your faith in God

Ezek. 33:10-19; 2 Cor. 13:5; Heb. 3:12; 2 Thess. 2:3;
1 Tim. 4:1; 2 Tim 4:4; 2 Pet. 2:20,3:17

DON'T FALL FROM GRACE !!!!!!!

Gal. 1:6-8,4:9-10,5:4; Heb. 12:15; Jude 3,4; Rev. 22:14-15

CHAPTER 3

DIVINE HEALING & HEALTH

There is divine healing and health for the inner person.

David's request for God to heal his inner-man

"I said, Lord, be merciful unto me: heal my soul; for I have sinned against thee." *(Ps. 41:4)*

God's invitation to salvation

"Therefore I will judge you, O house of Israel, every one according to his ways, saith the Lord God. Repent, and turn yourselves from all your transgressions; so iniquity shall not be your ruin.[31] Cast away from you all your transgressions, whereby ye have transgressed; and make you a new heart and a new spirit: for why will ye die, O house of Israel. [32] For I have no pleasure in the death of him that dieth, saith the Lord God: wherefore turn yourselves, and live ye." *(Ezek. 18:30-32)*

Jeremiah's understanding of the difference between healing of the body and soul

"Heal me, O Lord, and I shall be healed; save me, and I shall be saved: for thou art my praise." *(Jer. 17:14)*

One of many parables Jesus used to highlight 2 basic blessings for you
(Conversion of the inner man and healing of the body)

"Therefore speak I to them in parables: because they seeing see not; and hearing they hear not, neither do they understand. [14] And in them is fulfilled the prophecy of Esaias, which saith, By hearing ye shall hear, and shall not understand; and seeing ye shall see, and shall not perceive: [15] For this people's heart is waxed gross, and their ears are dull of hearing, and their eyes they have closed; lest at any time they should see with their eyes, and hear with their ears, and should understand with their heart, and should be converted, and I should heal them." (*Matt. 13:13-15*)

There is divine healing and health for the body

Jeremiah's cry of sorrow

"Is there no balm in Gilead; is there no physician there? why then is not the health of the daughter of my people recovered." *(Jer. 8:22)*

God's promise to His people

"For I will restore health unto thee, and I will heal thee of thy wounds, saith the Lord; because they called thee an Outcast, saying, This is Zion, whom no man seeketh after." *(Jer. 30:17)*

God's healing covenant based upon obedience to His word

"And said, If thou wilt diligently hearken to the voice of the Lord thy God, and wilt do that which is right in his sight, and wilt give ear to his commandments, and keep all his statutes, I will put none of these diseases upon thee, which I have brought upon the Egyptians: for I am the Lord that healeth thee." *(Ex. 15:26)*

Divine health

God's desire is for you to live out all of you years in divine health,until He calls you home.

"What man is he that desireth life, and loveth many days, that he may see good? [13] Keep thy tongue from evil, and thy lips from speaking guile. [14] Depart from evil, and do good; seek peace, and pursue it."
(Ps. 34:12-14)

"With long life will I satisfy him, and shew him my salvation." *(Ps. 91:16)*

"Beloved, I wish above all things that thou mayest prosper and be in health, even as thy soul prospereth." *(3 John 2)*

"For he that will love life, and see good days, let him refrain his tongue from evil, and his lips that they speak no guile: [11] Let him eschew evil, and do good; let him seek peace, and ensue it. [12] For the eyes of the Lord are over the righteous, and his ears are open unto their prayers: but the face of the Lord is against them that do evil." *(1 Pet. 3:10-12)*

David's acknowledgement of God as being the one who saves and heals

"Bless the Lord, O my soul, and forget not all his benefits: [3] Who forgiveth all thine iniquities; who healeth all thy diseases." *(Ps. 103:2-3)*

The prophet Isaiah's vision of Christ paying the price for divine healing and health before the death of Christ on the cross

"Surely he hath borne our griefs, and carried our sorrows: yet we did esteem him stricken, smitten of God, and afflicted. [5] But he was wounded for our transgressions, he was bruised for our iniquities: the chastisement of our peace was upon him; and with his stripes we are healed."
(Is. 53:4-5)

Peter echoing God's provision for healing of the body after the cross

"Who his own self bare our sins in his own body on the tree, that we, being dead to sins, should live unto righteousness: by whose stripes ye were healed." *(1 Pet. 2:24)*

God's answer for afflictions and sickness

"Is any sick among you? let him call for the elders of the church; and let them pray over him, anointing him with oil in the name of the Lord: [15] And the prayer of faith shall save the sick, and the Lord shall raise him up; and if he have committed sins, they shall be forgiven him. [16] Confess your faults one to another, and pray one for another, that ye may be healed. The effectual fervent prayer of a righteous man availeth much." *(James 5:14-16)*

For the Jews

"Make the heart of this people fat, and make their ears heavy, and shut their eyes; lest they see with their eyes, and hear with their ears, and understand with their heart, and convert, and be healed." *(Is. 6:10)*

Future healing of Israel

"Moreover the light of the moon shall be as the light of the sun, and the light of the sun shall be sevenfold, as the light of seven days, in the day that the Lord bindeth up the breach of his people, and healeth the stroke of their wound." *(Is. 30:26)*

For the Gentiles

"And the Lord shall smite Egypt: he shall smite and heal it: and they shall return even to the Lord, and he shall be intreated of them, and shall heal them." *(Is. 19:22)*

God's promise to heal both Jews and Gentiles who are righteous.

"I have seen his ways, and will heal him: I will lead him also, and restore comforts unto him and to his mourners. [19] I create the fruit of the lips; Peace, peace to him that is far off, and to him that is near, saith the Lord; and I will heal him." *(Is. 57:18-19)*

The woman who could not be healed by a physician

"And a woman having an issue of blood twelve years, which had spent all her living upon physicians, neither could be healed of any, [44] Came behind him, and touched the border of his garment: and immediately her issue of blood stanched. [45] And Jesus said, Who touched me? When all denied, Peter and they that were with him said, Master, the multitude throng thee and press thee, and sayest thou, Who touched me? [46] And Jesus said, Somebody hath touched me: for I perceive that virtue is gone out of me. [47] And when the woman saw that she was not hid, she came trembling, and falling down before him, she declared unto him before all the people for what cause she had touched him and how she was healed immediately. [48] And he said unto her, Daughter, be of good comfort: thy faith hath made thee whole; go in peace." *(Luke 8:43-48)*

You can get divine healing and health from God the same way you receive everything else from Him. Having faith and speaking the word.

"And Jesus answering saith unto them, Have faith in God. [23] For verily I say unto you, That whosoever shall say unto this mountain, Be thou removed, and be thou cast into the sea; and shall not doubt in his heart, but shall believe that those things which he saith shall come to pass; he shall have whatsoever he saith. [24] Therefore I say unto you, What things soever ye desire, when ye pray, believe that ye receive them, and ye shall have them." *(Mark 11:22-24)*

God's desire is that you are first converted (born again) and then healed from all sins, sickness, diseases and infirmities.

"And he said, Go, and tell this people, Hear ye indeed, but understand not; and see ye indeed, but perceive not. [10] Make the heart of this people fat, and make their ears heavy, and shut their eyes; lest they see with their eyes, and hear with their ears, and understand with their heart, and convert, and be healed." *(Is. 6:9-10)*

"Therefore speak I to them in parables: because they seeing see not; and hearing they hear not, neither do they understand. [14] And in them is fulfilled the prophecy of Esaias, which saith, By hearing ye shall hear, and shall not understand; and seeing ye shall see, and shall not perceive: [15] For this people's heart is waxed gross, and their ears are dull of hearing, and their eyes they have closed; lest at any time they should see with their eyes, and hear with their ears, and should understand with their heart, and should be converted, and I should heal them." *(Matt. 13:13-15)*

"He sent his word, and healed them, and delivered them from their destructions." *(Ps. 107:20)*

The Old Testament healing covenant in Ex. 15:26 was made part of the New Testament in Matt. 8:14-17. See additional references for details. Ps. 103:1-5,105:37,107:20; Is. 53:4-5; 1 Pet. 2:24; Gal. 3:13; 1 John 3:8; Rom. 8:11; Mark 16:17-18; John 14:12-15,15:7,16; Luke 8:40-48, 10:19, 13:10-17

In the following scriptures, Paul makes it very clear why many in the body of Christ are not receiving their physical healing. Pay specific attention to verses (29 and 30).

"After the same manner also he took the cup, when he had supped, saying, This cup is the new testament in my blood: this do ye, as oft as ye drink it, in remembrance of me. [26] For as often as ye eat this bread, and drink this cup, ye do shew the Lord's death till he come. [27] Wherefore whosoever shall eat this bread, and drink this cup of the Lord, unworthily, shall be guilty of the body and blood of the Lord. [28] But let a man examine himself, and so let him eat of that bread, and drink of that cup. [29] For he that eateth and drinketh unworthily, eateth and drinketh damnation to himself, not discerning the Lord's body. [30] For this cause many are weak and sickly among you, and many sleep." *(1 Cor. 11:25-30)*

Every time you partake in Holy Communion, you must celebrate the commemoration of the death, burial and resurrection of Jesus in its truest sense. One of the few things that God cannot do is, He cannot lie. Many are weak and sick in their bodies, simply because they are unworthily partaking of the finished work on the cross. Therefore, you must examine yourself and come to the expected conclusion of the matter and say: "By His stripes, I am healed".

THINGS MONEY CAN'T BUY

Whose report are you going to believe ?

"And what is the exceeding greatness of his power to us-ward who believe, according to the working of his mighty power, [20] Which he wrought in Christ, when he raised him from the dead, and set him at his own right hand in the heavenly places, Far above all principality, and power, and might, and dominion, and every name that is named, not only in this world, but also in that which is to come." *(Eph. 1:19-21)*

"Now unto him that is able to do exceeding abundantly above all that we ask or think, according to the power that worketh in us." *(Eph. 3:20)*

God's spoken words to His prophet Jeremiah

"Then came the word of the Lord unto Jeremiah, saying, [27] Behold, I am the Lord, the God of all flesh: is there any thing too hard for me?" *(Jer. 32:26-27)*

God promised all who would faithfully obey Him in Christ to supply all your needs. The apostle Paul made this very clear to the Philippians church.

"But my God shall supply all your need according to his riches in glory by Christ Jesus." *(Phil. 4:19)*

This word need comes from the Greek word Chreia "Khri-ah". Strongs #5532. It simply means that God will manifest in your life whatever you are lacking or wanting.

Your bodily healing was also provided for on the cross. See references. Ps. 103:1-3; Is. 53:4-5; Matt. 8:16-17; 1 Pet. 2:24; James 5:14-16 and the many scriptures enclosed for further details. As a child of God, you must learn to walk in the fullness of God's provisions.

Your deliverance in this area begins from a spiritual perspective. Ask God through the Holy Ghost to open up your understanding to 1 Cor. 11:25-30. The Holy Ghost will teach you how to worthily partake of the fullness of the Holy Communion.

Physical healing is a continuation of the work of Jesus. It is one of the children's promised provisions. The twelve disciples were commissioned to heal the sick (Luke 9:1-6). The seventy disciples were also commissioned to heal the sick (Luke 10:1,8-9,19). The early church continued the work of Jesus in their ministering of the gospel (Acts 3:1-10, 4:30, 5:16, 8:7, 9:34; 14:8-10, 19:11-12; Mark 16:18; 1 Cor. 12:9,28,30; James 5:14-16).

There are many ways (points of contact) in which God can heal your physical body through faith in His word. These are at least a few of them.

1. The laying on of hands. (Acts 9:17; Mark 16:14-20)

2. The repenting and confessing of sin along with the anointing of the sick person with oil. (Ps. 107:17-20; James 5:14-16)

3. The exercising of spiritual gifts. (1 Cor. 12:9)

4. Worship. (Ex. 23:25-26 NIV; Matt. 8:2-3, 15:22-28, 9:18,23-26)

5. Prayer of faith. (Mark 11:23-24; 2 Kgs. 20:1-11)

6. Communion. (1 Cor. 11:23-30)

7. Spoken word. (Job 22:28; Matt. 8:5-10,13:15)

8. Various means. Pauls' handkerchiefs. Acts 19:12; Jesus' garment. Matt. 9:20-22; Peter's shadow. Acts 5:14-16; Abraham's prayer. Gen.20:17; Elisha's intervening of the Shunammite's son. 2 Ki. 4:29-37; God's word. Ps. 107:20; Charitable giving. Ps. 41:1-3, 1 Cor. 11:22-30; Forgiveness. Ps. 103:1-3, Matt. 5:23-24, Mark 11:25, 1 Cor. 11:25-30, Eph. 4:27; A true fast. Is. chapter 58

God's promise for all things - even healing

"Again I say unto you, That if two of you shall agree on earth as touching any thing that they shall ask, it shall be done for them of my Father which is in heaven." *(Matt. 18:19)*

See other references. Ps. 66:18; 1 John 1:9; 2 Cor. 1:20; Rev. 22:2

CHAPTER 4

TRUE PROSPERITY

Job said that if you accumulate prosperity without it being a blessing from God, there will be seasons of great famine, in which the enemy will devour your dollars.

"In the fulness of his sufficiency he shall be in straits: every hand of the wicked shall come upon him." *(Job 20:22)*

James the brother of Jesus says:

"For the sun is no sooner risen with a burning heat, but it withereth the grass, and the flower thereof falleth, and the grace of the fashion of it perisheth: so also shall the rich man fade away in his ways. [12] Blessed is the man that endureth temptation: for when he is tried, he shall receive the crown of life, which the Lord hath promised to them that love him." *(James 1:11-12)*

True prosperity is not measured by the size of your financial portfolio. It is measured by your relationship and fellowship with your Lord and Saviour Jesus Christ – and your obedience to His commandments. See Luke 12:15.

The prophet Jeremiah says that you are truly prosperous when you place your full trust and hope in Jesus.

"Blessed is the man that trusteth in the Lord, and whose hope the Lord is. [8] For he shall be as a tree planted by the waters, and that spreadeth out her roots by the river, and shall not see when heat cometh, but her leaf shall be green; and shall not be careful in the year of drought, neither shall cease from yielding fruit." *(Jer. 17:7-8)*

TRUE PROSPERITY

David's evaluation of true prosperity

"Blessed is the man that walketh not in the counsel of the ungodly, nor standeth in the way of sinners, nor sitteth in the seat of the scornful. [2] But his delight is in the law of the Lord; and in his law doth he meditate day and night. [3] And he shall be like a tree planted by the rivers of water, that bringeth forth his fruit in his season; his leaf also shall not wither; and whatsoever he doeth shall prosper." *(Ps. 1:1-3)*

Jesus said: These are the blessed.

"And he opened his mouth, and taught them, saying, [3] Blessed are the poor in spirit: for theirs is the kingdom of heaven. [4] Blessed are they that mourn: for they shall be comforted. [5] Blessed are the meek: for they shall inherit the earth. [6] Blessed are they which do hunger and thirst after righteousness: for they shall be filled. [7] Blessed are the merciful: for they shall obtain mercy. [8] Blessed are the pure in heart: for they shall see God. [9] Blessed are the peacemakers: for they shall be called the children of God. [10] Blessed are they which are persecuted for righteousness' sake: for theirs is the kingdom of heaven. [11] Blessed are ye, when men shall revile you, and persecute you, and shall say all manner of evil against you falsely, for my sake. [12] Rejoice, and be exceeding glad: for great is your reward in heaven: for so persecuted they the prophets which were before you." *(Matt. 5:2-12)*

John the revelator says: These are the blessed ones.

"Blessed is he that readeth, and they that hear the words of this prophecy, and keep those things which are written therein: for the time is at hand." *(Rev. 1:3)*

True prosperity is knowing that you have Christ in you the hope of glory. This assurance allows you to look forward to the following eternal blessings from God.

THINGS MONEY CAN'T BUY

True eternal blessings of the redeemed.

1. Standing before God's heavenly throne.

"Therefore are they before the throne of God, and serve him day and night in his temple: and he that sitteth on the throne shall dwell among them." *(Rev. 7:15)*

2. Serving God day and night.

"Therefore are they before the throne of God, and serve him day and night in his temple: and he that sitteth on the throne shall dwell among them." *(Rev. 7:15)*

3. Always having the presence of God.

"Therefore are they before the throne of God, and serve him day and night in his temple: and he that sitteth on the throne shall dwell among them." *(Rev. 7:15)*

4. Never to hungry again.

"They shall hunger no more, neither thirst any more; neither shall the sun light on them, nor any heat." *(Rev. 7:16)*

5. Never to thirst any more.

"They shall hunger no more, neither thirst any more; neither shall the sun light on them, nor any heat." *(Rev. 7:16)*

6. Never to experience darkness again.

"They shall hunger no more, neither thirst any more; neither shall the sun light on them, nor any heat." *(Rev. 7:16)*

7. Never to be concern about the heat anymore.

"They shall hunger no more, neither thirst any more; neither shall the sun light on them, nor any heat." *(Rev. 7:16)*

8. Never to ever worry about your needs being met again.

"For the Lamb which is in the midst of the throne shall feed them, and shall lead them unto living fountains of waters: and God shall wipe away all tears from their eyes." *(Rev. 7:17)*

9. An everlasting source (supply) of fresh living waters.

"For the Lamb which is in the midst of the throne shall feed them, and shall lead them unto living fountains of waters: and God shall wipe away all tears from their eyes." *(Rev. 7:17)*

10. Never to sorrow again.

"For the Lamb which is in the midst of the throne shall feed them, and shall lead them unto living fountains of waters: and God shall wipe away all tears from their eyes." *(Rev. 7:17)*

"And I heard a great voice out of heaven saying, Behold, the tabernacle of God is with men, and he will dwell with them, and they shall be his people, and God himself shall be with them, and be their God. [4] And God shall wipe away all tears from their eyes; and there shall be no more death, neither sorrow, nor crying, neither shall there be any more pain: for the former things are passed away. [5] And he that sat upon the throne said, Behold, I make all things new. And he said unto me, Write: for these words are true and faithful. [6] And he said unto me, It is done. I am Alpha and Omega, the beginning and the end. I will give unto him that is athirst of the fountain of the water of life freely. [7] He that overcometh shall inherit all things; and I will be his God, and he shall be my son." *(Rev. 21:3-7)*

CHAPTER 5

TRUE SPIRITUAL RICHES

These blessings can not be bought with money. Christ has already paid for this in His sacrifice on the cross.

The pure in heart

"Blessed are the pure in heart: for they shall see God." *(Matt. 5:8)*

"Now it came to pass, as they went, that he entered into a certain village: and a certain woman named Martha received him into her house. [39] And she had a sister called Mary, which also sat at Jesus' feet, and heard his word. [40] But Martha was cumbered about much serving, and came to him, and said, Lord, dost thou not care that my sister hath left me to serve alone? bid her therefore that she help me. [41] And Jesus answered and said unto her, Martha, Martha, thou art careful and troubled about many things: [42] But one thing is needful: and Mary hath chosen that good part, which shall not be taken away from her." *(Luke 10:38-42)*

Mary had finally found what David had discovered. She finally realized that it is only in the presence of Jesus that one can experience the riches of God. Many are as Martha was. They have not found the true resting place - Being in the presence of the Lord.

"One thing have I desired of the Lord, that will I seek after; that I may dwell in the house of the Lord all the days of my life, to behold the beauty of the Lord, and to enquire in his temple." *(Ps. 27:4)*

"The day following Jesus would go forth into Galilee, and findeth Philip, and saith unto him, Follow me. [44] Now Philip was of Bethsaida, the city of Andrew and Peter. [45] Philip findeth Nathanael, and saith unto him, We have found him, of whom Moses in the law, and the prophets, did write, Jesus of Nazareth, the son of Joseph." *(John 1:43-45)*

"Yea doubtless, and I count all things but loss for the excellency of the knowledge of Christ Jesus my Lord: for whom I have suffered the loss of all things, and do count them but dung, that I may win Christ." *(Phil. 3:8)*

"Hearken, my beloved brethren, Hath not God chosen the poor of this world rich in faith, and heirs of the kingdom which he hath promised to them that love him." *(James 2:5)*

Paul's analogy of spiritual riches

"Blessed be the God and Father of our Lord Jesus Christ, who hath blessed us with all spiritual blessings in heavenly places in Christ." *(Eph. 1:3)*

Other spiritual riches (blessings) that can't be purchased with money.

1. Redemption through the blood of Jesus. Eph. 1:7
2. The word of God. Rom. 15:29
3. The grace of God. Acts 4:33
4. The mercy of God. Ps. 23:6,86:5,15,100:5,103:11,106:1,119:64, 145:8; Matt. 9:19; Eph. 2:4; 1 Pet. 1:3; Jude 1:21
5. The blessings of Abraham. Gen. 12:1-3; Gal. 3:14
6. The Holy Ghost. John 7:39; Gal. 3:14
7. Spiritual gifts. Rom. 1:11; 1 Cor. 12:1-11
8. Spiritual songs. Eph. 5:19
9. The Lord's Supper. 1 Cor. 10:16, 11:23-29
10. The riches of Christ. Eph. 3:8
11. The reproach of Christ. Heb. 11:26
12. The wisdom and knowledge of God. Rom. 11:33
13. The riches of God's goodness. Rom. 2:4
14. A righteous resurrection body. 1 Cor. 15:44-46
15. A spiritual harvest. Rom. 15:27; 1 Cor. 9:11
16. The fruit of the Spirit. Gal. 5:22-23
17. The riches of God's glory. Rom. 9:23; Eph. 3:16
18. The riches in God's glory. Phil. 4:19
19. The riches of the glory of Christ in you. Col. 1:27
20. God's glorious inheritance in the saints. Eph. 1:18
21. The Spirit of the Law (love). Rom. 7:14, 13:8-10

For blessings of obedience and curses of disobedience: See Heb. 6:7-8

Additional spiritual riches:

"For all the promises of God in him are yea, and in him Amen, unto the glory of God by us." *(2 Cor. 1:20)*

"And Jesus answering saith unto them, Have faith in God. [23] For verily I say unto you, That whosoever shall say unto this mountain, Be thou removed, and be thou cast into the sea; and shall not doubt in his heart, but shall believe that those things which he saith shall come to pass; he shall have whatsoever he saith. [24] Therefore I say unto you, What things soever ye desire, when ye pray, believe that ye receive them, and ye shall have them." *(Mark 11:22-24)*

"For the Lord God is a sun and shield: the Lord will give grace and glory: no good thing will he withhold from them that walk uprightly." *(Ps. 84:11)*

"O taste and see that the Lord is good: blessed is the man that trusteth in him. [9] O fear the Lord, ye his saints: for there is no want to them that fear him. [10] The young lions do lack, and suffer hunger: but they that seek the Lord shall not want any good thing." *(Ps. 34:8-10)*

"If ye abide in me, and my words abide in you, ye shall ask what ye will, and it shall be done unto you." *(John 15:7)*

Heavenly blessings (unlimited spiritual powers) in spiritual warfare

"That at the name of Jesus every knee should bow, of things in heaven, and things in earth, and things under the earth." *(Phil. 2:20)*

"And hath raised us up together, and made us sit together in heavenly places in Christ Jesus." *(Eph. 2:6)*

"For we wrestle not against flesh and blood, but against principalities, against powers, against the rulers of the darkness of this world, against spiritual wickedness in high places." *(Eph. 6:12)*

"The first man is of the earth, earthy: the second man is the Lord from heaven. [48] As is the earthy, such are they also that are earthy: and as is the heavenly, such are they also that are heavenly. [49] And as we have borne the image of the earthy, we hall also bear the image of the heavenly."
(1 Cor. 15:47-49)

"And the Lord shall deliver me from every evil work, and will preserve me unto his heavenly kingdom: to whom be glory for ever and ever. Amen."
(2 Tim. 4:18)

"To the intent that now unto the principalities and powers in heavenly places might be known by the church the manifold wisdom of God."
(Eph. 3:10)

"I counsel thee to buy of me gold tried in the fire, that thou mayest be rich; and white raiment, that thou mayest be clothed, and that the shame of thy nakedness do not appear; and anoint thine eyes with eyesalve, that thou mayest see." *(Rev. 3:18)*

CHAPTER 6

DELIVERANCE IN TIME OF GOD'S WRATH

"The integrity of the upright shall guide them: but the perverseness of transgressors shall destroy them. [4] Riches profit not in the day of wrath: but righteousness delivereth from death. [5] The righteousness of the perfect shall direct his way: but the wicked shall fall by his own wickedness. [6] The righteousness of the upright shall deliver them: but transgressors shall be taken in their own naughtiness. [7] When a wicked man dieth, his expectation shall perish: and the hope of unjust men perisheth. [8] The righteous is delivered out of trouble, and the wicked cometh in his stead."
(Prov. 11:3-8)

"He that trusteth in his riches shall fall: but the righteous shall flourish as a branch." *(Prov. 11:28)*

"Neither their silver nor their gold shall be able to deliver them in the day of the Lord's wrath; but the whole land shall be devoured by the fire of his jealousy: for he shall make even a speedy riddance of all them that dwell in the land." *(Zeph. 1:18)*

"For as a snare shall it come on all them that dwell on the face of the whole earth. [36] Watch ye therefore, and pray always, that ye may be accounted worthy to escape all these things that shall come to pass, and to stand before the Son of man." *(Luke 21:35-36)*

"And the kings of the earth, and the great men, and the rich men, and the chief captains, and the mighty men, and every bondman, and every free man, hid themselves in the dens and in the rocks of the mountains; [16] And said to the mountains and rocks, Fall on us, and hide us from the face of him that sitteth on the throne, and from the wrath of the Lamb: [17] For the great day of his wrath is come; and who shall be able to stand."
(Rev. 6:15-17)

DELIVERANCE IN TIME OF GOD'S WRATH

In the day of God's judgment, your money or wealth will not be able to deliver you from punishment. If your god has been your wealth, you and your god will perish together. Only the true righteousness of God in your life will be able to deliver you from eternal damnation.

John the revelator saw in the book of revelation what the end result would be for those whose name was not found written in the book of life.

"He that overcometh, the same shall be clothed in white raiment; and I will not blot out his name out of the book of life, but I will confess his name before my Father, and before his angels." *(Rev. 3:5)*

"And I saw the dead, small and great, stand before God; and the books were opened: and another book was opened, which is the book of life: and the dead were judged out of those things which were written in the books, according to their works. And whosoever was not found written in the book of life was cast into the lake of fire." *(Rev. 20:12,15)*

Future state of earthly possessions of the unrighteous

"The heaven shall reveal his iniquity; and the earth shall rise up against him. [28] The increase of his house shall depart, and his goods shall flow away in the day of his wrath." *(Job 20:27-28)*

Only the Blood of Jesus can deliver from the wrath to come

"For they themselves shew of us what manner of entering in we had unto you, and how ye turned to God from idols to serve the living and true God; [10] And to wait for his Son from heaven, whom he raised from the dead, even Jesus, which delivered us from the wrath to come. "
(1 Thess. 1:9-10)

Your houses of ivory (wealthy homes) or opulence (wealth, affluence) will not benefit you in the time of God's wrath (Amos 3:15).

CHAPTER 7

THE ASSURANCE OF TAKING IT WITH YOU AT DEATH

"Then Job arose, and rent his mantle, and shaved his head, and fell down upon the ground, and worshipped, And said, Naked came I out of my mother's womb, and naked shall I return thither: the Lord gave, and the Lord hath taken away; blessed be the name of the Lord." (*Job 1:20-21*)

"They take the timbrel and harp, and rejoice at the sound of the organ. [13] They spend their days in wealth, and in a moment go down to the grave." (*Job 21:12-13*)

"For he seeth that wise men die, likewise the fool and the brutish person perish, and leave their wealth to others." (*Ps. 49:10*)

"Be not thou afraid when one is made rich, when the glory of his house is increased; [17] For when he dieth he shall carry nothing away: his glory shall not descend after him." (*Ps. 49:16-17*)

"A good man leaveth an inheritance to his children's children: and the wealth of the sinner is laid up for the just." (*Prov. 13:22*)

The story of a certain rich man

"And he spake a parable unto them, saying, The ground of a certain rich man brought forth plentifully: [17] And he thought within himself, saying, What shall I do, because I have no room where to bestow my fruits? [18] And he said, This will I do: I will pull down my barns, and build greater; and there will I bestow all my fruits and my goods. [19] And I will say to my soul, Soul, thou hast much goods laid up for many years; take thine ease, eat, drink, and be merry. [20] But God said unto him, Thou fool, this night thy soul shall be required of thee: then whose shall those things be, which thou hast provided? [21] So is he that layeth up treasure for himself, and is not rich toward God." (*Luke 12:16-21*)

It would be a wise idea to prepare you a will.

"A good man leaveth an inheritance to his children's children: and the wealth of the sinner is laid up for the just." *(Prov. 13:22)* See Prov. 22:6

However, you should take this into consideration.

"To the chief Musician upon Mahalath, Maschil, A Psalm of David. The fool hath said in his heart, There is no God. Corrupt are they, and have done abominable iniquity: there is none that doeth good." *(Ps. 53:1)*

The story of a sad rich man

"And he said unto them, Take heed, and beware of covetousness: for a man's life consisteth not in the abundance of the things which he possesseth. [16] And he spake a parable unto them, saying, The ground of a certain rich man brought forth plentifully: [17] And he thought within himself, saying, What shall I do, because I have no room where to bestow my fruits? [18] And he said, This will I do: I will pull down my barns, and build greater; and there will I bestow all my fruits and my goods. [19] And I will say to my soul, Soul, thou hast much goods laid up for many years; take thine ease, eat, drink, and be merry. [20] But God said unto him, Thou fool, this night thy soul shall be required of thee: then whose shall those things be, which thou hast provided? [21] So is he that layeth up treasure for himself, and is not rich toward God." *(Luke 12:15-21)*

"The wise in heart will receive commandments: but a prating fool shall fall." *(Prov. 10:8)*

"The way of a fool is right in his own eyes: but he that hearkeneth unto counsel is wise." *(Prov. 12:15)*

"A wise man feareth, and departeth from evil: but the fool rageth, and is confident." *(Prov. 14:16)*

"A fool despiseth his father's instruction: but he that regardeth reproof is prudent." *(Prov. 15:5)*

"A fool hath no delight in understanding, but that his heart may discover itself." (*Prov. 18:2*)

"The heart is deceitful above all things, and desperately wicked: who can know it? [10] I the Lord search the heart, I try the reins, even to give every man according to his ways, and according to the fruit of his doings. [11] As the partridge sitteth on eggs, and hatcheth them not; so he that getteth riches, and not by right, shall leave them in the midst of his days, and at his end shall be a fool." *(Jer. 17:9-11)*

"But godliness with contentment is great gain. [7] For we brought nothing into this world, and it is certain we can carry nothing out." *(1 Tim. 6:6-7)*

The story of Lazarus and the rich man

"There was a certain rich man, which was clothed in purple and fine linen, and fared sumptuously every day: [20] And there was a certain beggar named Lazarus, which was laid at his gate, full of sores, [21] And desiring to be fed with the crumbs which fell from the rich man's table: moreover the dogs came and licked his sores. [22] And it came to pass, that the beggar died, and was carried by the angels into Abraham's bosom: the rich man also died, and was buried; [23] And in hell he lift up his eyes, being in torments, and seeth Abraham afar off, and Lazarus in his bosom. [24] And he cried and said, Father Abraham, have mercy on me, and send Lazarus, that he may dip the tip of his finger in water, and cool my tongue; for I am tormented in this flame. [25] But Abraham said, Son, remember that thou in thy lifetime receivedst thy good things, and likewise Lazarus evil things: but now he is comforted, and thou art tormented." *(Luke 16:19-25)*

The words of Job

"For what is the hope of the hypocrite, though he hath gained, when God taketh away his soul?" *(Job 27:8)*

See other references. Ps. 39:6; Eccl. 2:18,21

CHAPTER 8

TRUE LOVE

Love is simply a commitment that one person has for another. A commitment can't be bought. However, a feeling can be bought and manipulated.

In the following scripture, Solomon stated that you would be better off having a little and true love – than having an abundance with no love and much enmity.

"Better is a dinner of herbs where love is, than a stalled ox and hatred therewith." (*Prov. 15:17*)

I must reflect on the biblical story that the Lord gave me for this chapter in the book.

God made king Solomon the richest man to live outside His Son Jesus. Even with all the riches of the world, Solomon could not buy the loyal love of the shulamite woman.

"Set me as a seal upon thine heart, as a seal upon thine arm: for love is strong as death; jealousy is cruel as the grave: the coals thereof are coals of fire, which hath a most vehement flame. Many waters cannot quench love, neither can the floods drown it: if a man would give all the substance of his house for love, it would utterly be contemned." (*Song 8:6-7*)

Solomon describes below the characteristics of true love.

1. Sealed with God's stamp of approval.

"Wherefore they are no more twain, but one flesh. What therefore God hath joined together, let not man put asunder." (*Matt. 19:6*)

2. Strong. As the grave will not give up the dead. True love will not surrender to death (separation), because it is bound together by the three-fold cord of God.

This three-fold cord consists of: The man, his wife and High Priest (Jesus). Remember the following words from Paul on love.

"For I am persuaded, that neither death, nor life, nor angels, nor principalities, nor powers, nor things present, nor things to come, [39] Nor height, nor depth, nor any other creature, shall be able to separate us from the love of God, which is in Christ Jesus our Lord." *(Rom. 8:38-39)*

3. Indestructible. As the spirit of jealousy and the grave are very cruelly strong, with constant flames of evilness, the indwelling fire of the Holy Ghost will always possess the power of true love to quench the flames of evilness to allow you to stand the test of times.

Remember, God will always bring you through the fire

"When thou passest through the waters, I will be with thee; and through the rivers, they shall not overflow thee: when thou walkest through the fire, thou shalt not be burned; neither shall the flame kindle upon thee."
(Is. 43:2) See also. Is. 43:14-17,19; 1 John 4:4

4. Unquenchable. This characteristic simply means that whatever weapons the enemy tries to use to put out the foundational flames of true love, God will not allow him to succeed. No weapon can quench God's flaming fire.

Always, remember the words of David

"I will exalt you, O LORD, for you lifted me out of the depths and did not let my enemies gloat over me." *(Ps. 30:1 NIV)*

Remember, God will always bring you through the water and floods

"When thou passest through the waters, I will be with thee; and through the rivers, they shall not overflow thee: when thou walkest through the fire, thou shalt not be burned; neither shall the flame kindle upon thee."
(Is. 43:2) See also. Is. 43:14-17,19

5. Invaluable. A person who does not fear and understand God - will place the value of money over true love. In other words, he or she will allow money to be the number one factor in a relationship. A word of wisdom from God. It is in Him you live, move and have your entire being (see Acts 17:28; Heb. 1:3). Seek first the kingdom of God and His righteousness. Then, all of the things that pertain to godliness will be freely given to you. Hallelujah!

Why ?

"For ye know the grace of our Lord Jesus Christ, that, though he was rich, yet for your sakes he became poor, that ye through his poverty might be rich." *(2 Cor 8:9)*

Remember also.

"For thou shalt worship no other god: for the Lord, whose name is Jealous, is a jealous God." *(Ex. 34:14)*

The following reference shows you how the shulamite woman rejects Solomon for her fiancé, the one she had promised her love to.

"I am my beloved's, and his desire is toward me. [11] Come, my beloved, let us go forth into the field; let us lodge in the villages. [12] Let us get up early to the vineyards; let us see if the vine flourish, whether the tender grape appear, and the pomegranates bud forth: there will I give thee my loves. [13] The mandrakes give a smell, and at our gates are all manner of pleasant fruits, new and old, which I have laid up for thee, O my beloved." *(Song 7:10-13)*

Read the entire book of the Song of Solomon for a better picture.

In Paul's first letter to the Corinthians, he reminded them of the non-effect of the spiritual gifts, if love were not the foundational principal. He also discussed the many characteristics of true love.

"Charity suffereth long, and is kind; charity envieth not; charity vaunteth not itself, is not puffed up, [5] Doth not behave itself unseemly, seeketh not her own, is not easily provoked, thinketh no evil; [6] Rejoiceth not in iniquity, but rejoiceth in the truth; [7] Beareth all things, believeth all things, hopeth all things, endureth all things. [8] Charity never faileth: but whether there be prophecies, they shall fail; whether there be tongues, they shall cease; whether there be knowledge, it shall vanish away. [9] For we know in part, and we prophesy in part. [10] But when that which is perfect is come, then that which is in part shall be done away. [11] When I was a child, I spake as a child, I understood as a child, I thought as a child: but when I became a man, I put away childish things. [12] For now we see through a glass, darkly; but then face to face: now I know in part; but then shall I know even as also I am known. [13] And now abideth faith, hope, charity, these three; but the greatest of these is charity." *(1 Cor. 13:4-13)*

True love surely can't be purchase with money. Money is a tangible temporary thing. Love is God. He is from everlasting to everlasting, and can't be bought. True love is the agape (unconditional or divine) type love.

Other types of love

Where conditions may be attached

Phileo - Friendship type love.

Eros - Physical type love.

Storge - Family members type love.

CHAPTER 9

SPIRITUAL GIFTS

The Holy Ghost is the first fruit gift for the believer. It is God's desire that every believer receives this precious gift.

"Which is the earnest of our inheritance until the redemption of the purchased possession, unto the praise of his glory." *(Eph. 1:14)*

"If ye then, being evil, know how to give good gifts unto your children: how much more shall your heavenly Father give the Holy Spirit to them that ask him?" *(Luke 11:13)*

James said of these gifts

"Every good gift and every perfect gift is from above, and cometh down from the Father of lights, with whom is no variableness, neither shadow of turning." *(James 1:17)*

Let us look at how these gifts are received.

Motivational gifts are from the Father

"Having then gifts differing according to the grace that is <u>given</u> to us, whether prophecy, let us prophesy according to the proportion of faith; [7] Or ministry, let us wait on our ministering: or he that teacheth, on teaching; [8] Or he that exhorteth, on exhortation: he that giveth, let him do it with simplicity; he that ruleth, with diligence; he that sheweth mercy, with cheerfulness." *(Rom. 12:6-8)*

"Train up a child in the way he should go: and when he is old, he will not depart from it." *(Prov. 22:6)*

"For thou hast possessed my reins: thou hast covered me in my mother's womb. [14] I will praise thee; for I am fearfully and wonderfully made: marvellous are thy works; and that my soul knoweth right well. [15] My substance was not hid from thee, when I was made in secret, and curiously wrought in the lowest parts of the earth. [16] Thine eyes did see my substance, yet being unperfect; and in thy book all my members were written, which in continuance were fashioned, when as yet there was none of them." *(Ps. 139:13-16)*

Ministry gifts are from the Son

"And he <u>gave</u> some, apostles; and some, prophets; and some, evangelists; and some, pastors and teachers; [12] For the perfecting of the saints, for the work of the ministry, for the edifying of the body of Christ: [13] Till we all come in the unity of the faith, and of the knowledge of the Son of God, unto a perfect man, unto the measure of the stature of the fulness of Christ: [14] That we henceforth be no more children, tossed to and fro, and carried about with every wind of doctrine, by the sleight of men, and cunning craftiness, whereby they lie in wait to deceive." *(Eph. 4:11-14)*

Manifestation gifts are from the Holy Ghost

"But the manifestation of the Spirit is given to every man to profit withal. [8] For to one is <u>given</u> by the Spirit the word of wisdom; to another the word of knowledge by the same Spirit; [9] To another faith by the same Spirit; to another the gifts of healing by the same Spirit; [10] To another the working of miracles; to another prophecy; to another discerning of spirits; to another divers kinds of tongues; to another the interpretation of tongues."
(1 Cor. 12:7-10)

Let us look at an example of someone who tried to buy the gift of the Holy Ghost.

Simon the sorcerer

"Now when the apostles which were at Jerusalem heard that Samaria had received the word of God, they sent unto them Peter and John: [15] Who, when they were come down, prayed for them, that they might receive the Holy Ghost: [16] (For as yet he was fallen upon none of them: only they were baptized in the name of the Lord Jesus.) [17] Then laid they their hands on them, and they received the Holy Ghost. [18] And when Simon saw that through laying on of the apostles' hands the Holy Ghost was given, he offered them money, [19] Saying, Give me also this power, that on whomsoever I lay hands, he may receive the Holy Ghost. [20] But Peter said unto him, Thy money perish with thee, because thou hast thought that the gift of God may be purchased with money. [21] Thou hast neither part nor lot in this matter: for thy heart is not right in the sight of God. [22] Repent therefore of this thy wickedness, and pray God, if perhaps the thought of thine heart may be forgiven thee. [23] For I perceive that thou art in the gall of bitterness, and in the bond of iniquity. [24] Then answered Simon, and said, Pray ye to the Lord for me, that none of these things which ye have spoken come upon me." *(Acts 8:14-24)*

CHAPTER 10

DIVINE POWER (Anointing of God)

"But thou shalt remember the Lord thy God: for it is he that giveth thee power to get wealth, that he may establish his covenant which he sware unto thy fathers, as it is this day." *(Deut. 8:18)*

As you see in the above reference, it is God himself who gives you power, even to get wealth. It is when you misuse or abuse this power with wealth or any other thing that you sin against God. Never forget the fact that God is your source, not your resource. Everything else is your resource, including the money and occupation.

The power of God without measure has been promised to all believers. Ezek. 36:26-27; Matt. 18:18; Luke 11:13,24:49; Acts 1:4,8, 2:38-39; John 7:37-39.

Why without measure ? Because, if Jesus needed the Spirit without measure to do the works He did, surely, you are going to need at least what He had to continue where He left off. No doubt you will need the anointing without measure to do the greater works than Jesus did.

By the way, the power of God is just one of His many attributes. Below you will see a few ways in which His power is manifested.

You should be mindful that the anointed power of God without measure is not for non-believers.

"Even the Spirit of truth; whom the world cannot receive, because it seeth him not, neither knoweth him: but ye know him; for he dwelleth with you, and shall be in you." *(John 14:17)*

Through God himself

"God hath spoken once; twice have I heard this; that power belongeth unto God." *(Ps. 62:11)*

"But Jesus beheld them, and said unto them, With men this is impossible; but with God all things are possible." *(Matt. 19:26)*

"He ruleth by his power for ever; his eyes behold the nations: let not the rebellious exalt themselves. Selah." *(Ps. 66:7)* See also. Ps. 28:8,89:19-20

"But we have this treasure in earthen vessels, that the excellency of the power may be of God, and not of us." *(2 Cor. 4:7)*

"Which he wrought in Christ, when he raised him from the dead, and set him at his own right hand in the heavenly places, [21] Far above all principality, and power, and might, and dominion, and every name that is named, not only in this world, but also in that which is to come: [22] And hath put all things under his feet, and gave him to be the head over all things to the church, [23] Which is his body, the fulness of him that filleth all in all." *(Eph. 1:20-23)*

"How God anointed Jesus of Nazareth with the Holy Ghost and with power: who went about doing good, and healing all that were oppressed of the devil; for God was with him." *(Acts 10:38)* See also. Matt. 3:16-17

Through the Father

"Therefore we are buried with him by baptism into death: that like as Christ was raised up from the dead by the glory of the Father, even so we also should walk in newness of life." *(Rom. 6:4)*

Through the Son

"For by him were all things created, that are in heaven, and that are in earth, visible and invisible, whether they be thrones, or dominions, or principalities, or powers: all things were created by him, and for him: [17] And he is before all things, and by him all things consist." *(Col. 1:16-17)* See also. John 1:12; Matt. 3:11

"Who being the brightness of his glory, and the express image of his person, and upholding all things by the word of his power, when he had by himself purged our sins, sat down on the right hand of the Majesty on high." *(Heb. 1:3)*

"Behold, I give unto you power to tread on serpents and scorpions, and over all the power of the enemy: and nothing shall by any means hurt you." *(Luke 10:19)*

"I can do all things through Christ which strengtheneth me." *(Phil. 4:13)*
See also. Matt. 28:18; 1 Cor 1:24; Eph. 3:10; Col. 2:9-10

Through the Holy Ghost

"Then he said unto me, Son of man, these bones are the whole house of Israel: behold, they say, Our bones are dried, and our hope is lost: we are cut off for our parts. [12] Therefore prophesy and say unto them, Thus saith the Lord God; Behold, O my people, I will open your graves, and cause you to come up out of your graves, and bring you into the land of Israel. [13] And ye shall know that I am the Lord, when I have opened your graves, O my people, and brought you up out of your graves, [14] And shall put my spirit in you, and ye shall live, and I shall place you in your own land: then shall ye know that I the Lord have spoken it, and performed it, saith the Lord." *(Ezek. 37:11-14)*

"The Spirit of the Lord is upon me, because he hath anointed me to preach the gospel to the poor; he hath sent me to heal the brokenhearted, to preach deliverance to the captives, and recovering of sight to the blind, to set at liberty them that are bruised, [19] to preach the acceptable year of the Lord." *(Luke 4:18-19)*

"But if the Spirit of him that raised up Jesus from the dead dwell in you, he that raised up Christ from the dead shall also quicken your mortal bodies by his Spirit that dwelleth in you." *(Rom. 8:11)*

"But if I cast out devils by the Spirit of God, then the kingdom of God is come unto you." *(Matt. 12:28)*

"And Jesus returned in the power of the Spirit into Galilee: and there went out a fame of him through all the region round about." *(Luke 4:14)*

"But ye shall receive power, after that the Holy Ghost is come upon you: and ye shall be witnesses unto me both in Jerusalem, and in all Judaea, and in Samaria, and unto the uttermost part of the earth." *(Acts 1:8)*

See also. 1 Cor. 2:4-5; Eph. 3:16

Through the word

"For I am not ashamed of the gospel of Christ: for it is the power of God unto salvation to every one that believeth; to the Jew first, and also to the Greek." *(Rom 1:16)*

"In whom ye also trusted, after that ye heard the word of truth, the gospel of your salvation: in whom also after that ye believed, ye were sealed with that Holy Spirit of promise." *(Eph. 1:13)*

See additional references. 1 Cor 1:18-24; Acts 10:44,11:15, 20:32; Eph. 6:17; Heb. 4:12; Rom. 15:29

Through spiritual gifts

"For the perfecting of the saints, for the work of the ministry, for the edifying of the body of Christ: [13] Till we all come in the unity of the faith, and of the knowledge of the Son of God, unto a perfect man, unto the measure of the stature of the fulness of Christ: [14] That we henceforth be no more children, tossed to and fro, and carried about with every wind of doctrine, by the sleight of men, and cunning craftiness, whereby they lie in wait to deceive; [15] But speaking the truth in love, may grow up into him in all things, which is the head, even Christ: [16] From whom the whole body fitly joined together and compacted by that which every joint supplieth, according to the effectual working in the measure of every part, maketh increase of the body unto the edifying of itself in love." *(Eph. 4:12-16)*

Through praying in the Holy Ghost

"For this cause I bow my knees unto the Father of our Lord Jesus Christ. That he would grant you, according to the riches of his glory, to be strengthened with might by his Spirit in the inner man." *(Eph. 3:14,16)*

"Praying always with all prayer and supplication in the Spirit, and watching thereunto with all perseverance and supplication for all saints." *(Eph. 6:18)*

"But ye, beloved, building up yourselves on your most holy faith, praying in the Holy Ghost." *(Jude 1:20)* See also. Zech. 12:10; Rom. 8:26-27

Through true fasting

"Wherefore have we fasted, say they, and thou seest not? wherefore have we afflicted our soul, and thou takest no knowledge? Behold, in the day of your fast ye find pleasure, and exact all your labours. [4] Behold, ye fast for strife and debate, and to smite with the fist of wickedness: ye shall not fast as ye do this day, to make your voice to be heard on high. [5] Is it such a fast that I have chosen? a day for a man to afflict his soul? is it to bow down his head as a bulrush, and to spread sackcloth and ashes under him? wilt thou call this a fast, and an acceptable day to the Lord? [6] Is not this the fast that I have chosen? to loose the bands of wickedness, to undo the heavy burdens, and to let the oppressed go free, and that ye break every yoke?" *(Is. 58:3-6)*

All believers are anointed by God, with a measure of the anointing at conversion.

"But as many as received him, to them gave he power to become the sons of God, even to them that believe on his name." *(John 1:12)*

"Now he which stablisheth us with you in Christ, and hath anointed us, is God; [22] Who hath also sealed us, and given the earnest of the Spirit in our hearts." *(2 Cor. 1:21-22)*

Through the glory

"Then sang Moses and the children of Israel this song unto the Lord, and spake, saying, I will sing unto the Lord, for he hath triumphed gloriously: the horse and his rider hath he thrown into the sea." *(Ex. 15:1)*

"Therefore we are buried with him by baptism into death: that like as Christ was raised up from the dead by the glory of the Father, even so we also should walk in newness of life." *(Rom. 6:4)*

"The heavens declare the glory of God; and the firmament sheweth his handywork." *(Ps. 19:1)*

"His work is honourable and glorious: and his righteousness endureth for ever." *(Ps. 111:3)*

Through trails and tribulations

"And he said unto me, My grace is sufficient for thee: for my strength is made perfect in weakness. Most gladly therefore will I rather glory in my infirmities, that the power of Christ may rest upon me." (2 Cor. 12:9)

Through impartation

"For I long to see you, that I may impart unto you some spiritual gift, to the end ye may be established." *(Rom. 1:11)*

Through the laying on of hands

"And when Simon saw that through laying on of the apostles' hands the Holy Ghost was given, he offered them money." *(Acts 8:18)* See also. Acts 9:17,19:1-7

THINGS MONEY CAN'T BUY

Remember, after you are anointed with a measure of power at conversion, you must wait until you are endued with the fullness of the anointing to begin to do the greater works than Jesus.

In the book of Luke 4:18-19, Jesus describes what the power of God equipped Him to do. You to must understand where true power comes from and the things it can accomplish. All the money in the world will not qualify you to do the following.

Firstly. You must know that you have experienced the Jordan river opening of heaven and the power of God descending upon you – God's mantle descending upon you – and growing strong in the Spirit. God will then command you, as He did Moses - Tell Pharaoh to let my people go.

You must only go in the power of the Spirit. See also. Zech. 4:6; Micah 3:8; Rom. 15:19; Eph. 6:10

Then: You will be able to do the following.

1. Preach the gospel. To evangelize the gospel of the grace of God. John 8:31-36

2. Heal the brokenhearted. Ps. 147:3; Luke 4:18; Acts 10:38

3. Preach deliverance to the captives. Those that are bound by the enemy in all sorts of areas. Especially those that allow money to be their god. Eph 4:7-11; Heb. 2:14-15

4. Heal the sick. Matt. 10:8

5. Set at liberty them that are bruised. Is. 58:6-14

6. Preach the acceptable year of the Lord. Proclaiming the liberation from the law of sin, death and all of their consequences. 2 Cor. 6:2; Rom. 8:2; Heb. 2:14-15

The anointing brings deliverance

"And it shall come to pass in that day, that his burden shall be taken away from off thy shoulder, and his yoke from off thy neck, and the yoke shall be destroyed because of the anointing." *(Is. 10:27)*

Paul's understanding of the source of real power

"Hath not the potter power over the clay, of the same lump to make one vessel unto honour, and another unto dishonour." (Rom. 9:21)

Learn to wait on God

"And God is able to make all grace abound toward you; that ye, always having all sufficiency in all things, may abound to every good work."
(2 Cor. 9:8)

"But truly I am full of power by the spirit of the Lord, and of judgment, and of might, to declare unto Jacob his transgression, and to Israel his sin."
(Mic. 3:8)

"But as many as received him, to them gave he power to become the sons of God, even to them that believe on his name." *(John 1:12)*

"Behold, I give unto you power to tread on serpents and scorpions, and over all the power of the enemy: and nothing shall by any means hurt you."
(Luke 10:19)

"And, behold, I send the promise of my Father upon you: but tarry ye in the city of Jerusalem, until ye be endued with power from on high."
(Luke 24:49)

"In the last day, that great day of the feast, Jesus stood and cried, saying, If any man thirst, let him come unto me, and drink. [38] He that believeth on me, as the scripture hath said, out of his belly shall flow rivers of living water. [39] (But this spake he of the Spirit, which they that believe on him should receive: for the Holy Ghost was not yet given; because that Jesus was not yet glorified)." *(John 7:37-39)*

"But ye shall receive power, after that the Holy Ghost is come upon you: and ye shall be witnesses unto me both in Jerusalem, and in all Judaea, and in Samaria, and unto the uttermost part of the earth." *(Acts 1:8)*

"Now unto him that is able to do exceeding abundantly above all that we ask or think, according to the power that worketh in us." *(Eph. 3:20)*

"Whereby are given unto us exceeding great and precious promises: that by these ye might be partakers of the divine nature, having escaped the corruption that is in the world through lust." *(2 Pet. 1:4)*

"Finally, my brethren, be strong in the Lord, and in the power of his might." *(Eph. 6:10)*

This anointed power has already been provided for by God. God wants every believer to partake of this same power, just by walking in obedience to His word.

"What shall we say then? Shall we continue in sin, that grace may abound? [2] God forbid. How shall we, that are dead to sin, live any longer therein? [3] Know ye not, that so many of us as were baptized into Jesus Christ were baptized into his death? [4] Therefore we are buried with him by baptism into death: that like as Christ was raised up from the dead by the glory of the Father, even so we also should walk in newness of life. [5] For if we have been planted together in the likeness of his death, we shall be also in the likeness of his resurrection: [6] Knowing this, that our old man is crucified with him, that the body of sin might be destroyed, that henceforth we should not serve sin. [7] For he that is dead is freed from sin. [8] Now if we be dead with Christ, we believe that we shall also live with him." *(Rom. 6:1-8)*

Once you have received the anointing of God without measure as Jesus did, you can fulfill the following command.

"Verily, verily, I say unto you, He that believeth on me, the works that I do shall he do also; and greater works than these shall he do; because I go unto my Father." *(John 14:12)*

You must always walk in the fullness of the anointing in the Spirit. Whenever you feel as though you need a fresh anointing, one of the things you can do is to do what the disciples did.

"And now, Lord, behold their threatenings: and grant unto thy servants, that with all boldness they may speak thy word, [30] By stretching forth thine hand to heal; and that signs and wonders may be done by the name of thy holy child Jesus. [31] And when they had prayed, the place was shaken where they were assembled together; and they were all filled with the Holy Ghost, and they spake the word of God with boldness."
(Acts 4:29-31)

See additional references. John 1:16; Phil. 1:19; 2 Cor. 1:22,5:5; Eph. 3:19; 1 John 4:13; Gal. 5:16-26

The anointing (power of God) can't be bought with money. Below is an example of someone trying to buy the power of God.

"But there was a certain man, called Simon, which beforetime in the same city used sorcery, and bewitched the people of Samaria, giving out that himself was some great one: [10] To whom they all gave heed, from the least to the greatest, saying, This man is the great power of God. [11] And to him they had regard, because that of long time he had bewitched them with sorceries. [12] But when they believed Philip preaching the things concerning the kingdom of God, and the name of Jesus Christ, they were baptized, both men and women. [13] Then Simon himself believed also: and when he was baptized, he continued with Philip, and wondered, beholding the miracles and signs which were done. [14] Now when the apostles which were at Jerusalem heard that Samaria had received the word of God, they sent unto them Peter and John: [15] Who, when they were come down, prayed for them, that they might receive the Holy Ghost: [16] (For as yet he was fallen upon none of them: only they were baptized in the name of the Lord Jesus.)

[17] Then laid they their hands on them, and they received the Holy Ghost. [18] And when Simon saw that through laying on of the apostles' hands the Holy Ghost was given, he offered them money, [19] Saying, Give me also this power, that on whomsoever I lay hands, he may receive the Holy Ghost. [20] But Peter said unto him, Thy money perish with thee, because thou hast thought that the gift of God may be purchased with money. [21] Thou hast neither part nor lot in this matter: for thy heart is not right in the sight of God." *(Acts 8:9-21)*

CHAPTER 11

JOY (Jesus on You - Gal. 3:27)

The word joy comes from the Greek words Chara "khar-ah" and Chairo. It simply means cheerfulness, calm delight and gladness.

Why Joy? It is the strength for the child of God

"Then he said unto them, Go your way, eat the fat, and drink the sweet, and send portions unto them for whom nothing is prepared: for this day is holy unto our Lord: neither be ye sorry; for the joy of the Lord is your strength." *(Neh. 8:10)*

Every believer should live a joyful life. Sadly, many believers do not realize that this blessing has also been paid for by Christ.

Joy has been promised to all of God's children

"Light is sown for the righteous, and gladness for the upright in heart." *(Ps. 97:11)*

"I will also clothe her priests with salvation: and her saints shall shout aloud for joy." *(Ps. 132:16)*

See additional references. Is. 35:10; 55:12; 56:7

Let's look at the true source of joy

"For God giveth to a man that is good in his sight wisdom, and knowledge, and joy: but to the sinner he giveth travail, to gather and to heap up, that he may give to him that is good before God. This also is vanity and vexation of spirit." *(Eccl. 2:26)*

"In thy name shall they rejoice all the day: and in thy righteousness shall they be exalted." *(Ps. 89:16)*

"Let Israel rejoice in him that made him: let the children of Zion be joyful in their King." *(Ps. 149:2)*

"Yet I will rejoice in the Lord, I will joy in the God of my salvation." *(Hab. 3:18)*

"And not only so, but we also joy in God through our Lord Jesus Christ, by whom we have now received the atonement." *(Rom. 5:11)*

Joy also can be found in different manifestations of God.

In Jesus

"And my spirit hath rejoiced in God my Saviour." *(Luke 1:47)*

"For we are the circumcision, which worship God in the spirit, and rejoice in Christ Jesus, and have no confidence in the flesh." *(Phil. 3:3)*

The more Jesus is manifested in your life, the more joy you will have.

"If ye keep my commandments, ye shall abide in my love; even as I have kept my Father's commandments, and abide in his love. [11] These things have I spoken unto you, that my joy might remain in you, and that your joy might be full." *(John 15:10-11)*

In the Holy Ghost

"For the kingdom of God is not meat and drink; but righteousness, and peace, and joy in the Holy Ghost." *(Rom. 14:17)*

In seeking God

"Let all those that seek thee rejoice and be glad in thee: and let such as love thy salvation say continually, Let God be magnified." *(Ps. 70:4)*

THINGS MONEY CAN'T BUY

In the word of God

"Thy words were found, and I did eat them; and thy word was unto me the joy and rejoicing of mine heart: for I am called by thy name, O Lord God of hosts." *(Jer. 15:16)*

See additional references. Neh. 8:12; Ps. 119:111-116, 119:47,97,162

As preached by Jesus.

"And now come I to thee; and these things I speak in the world, that they might have my joy fulfilled in themselves. [14] I have given them thy word; and the world hath hated them, because they are not of the world, even as I am not of the world. *(John 17:13-14)*

In the fellowship of the saints

"And the children of Israel, which were come again out of captivity, and all such as had separated themselves unto them from the filthiness of the heathen of the land, to seek the Lord God of Israel, did eat, And kept the feast of unleavened bread seven days with joy: for the Lord had made them joyful, and turned the heart of the king of Assyria unto them, to strengthen their hands in the work of the house of God, the God of Israel." *(Ezra 6:21-22)*

"When I remember these things, I pour out my soul in me: for I had gone with the multitude, I went with them to the house of God, with the voice of joy and praise, with a multitude that kept holyday." *(Ps. 42:4)*

Paul's letter to Timothy.

"To Timothy, my dearly beloved son: Grace, mercy, and peace, from God the Father and Christ Jesus our Lord. [3] I thank God, whom I serve from my forefathers with pure conscience, that without ceasing I have remembrance of thee in my prayers night and day. Greatly desiring to see thee, being mindful of thy tears, that I may be filled with joy." *(2 Tim. 1:2-4)*
See additional reference. 2 John 1:12

Even in giving

"Then the people rejoiced, for that they offered willingly, because with perfect heart they offered willingly to the Lord: and David the king also rejoiced with great joy." *(1 Chr. 29:9,17)*   See also. Ps. 126:5-6

In God's glory

"But rejoice, inasmuch as ye are partakers of Christ's sufferings; that, when his glory shall be revealed, ye may be glad also with exceeding joy."
(1 Pet. 4:13)

Received from singing spiritual songs

"Speaking to yourselves in psalms and hymns and spiritual songs, singing and making melody in your heart to the Lord." *(Eph. 5:19)*

"Is any among you afflicted? let him pray. Is any merry? let him sing psalms." *(James 5:13)*

In speaking the word

"A man hath joy by the answer of his mouth: and a word spoken in due season, how good is it!" *(Prov. 15:23)* See also. Prov. 12:14

Joy can't be purchased with temporal things such as money.

Solomon knew this.

"And whatsoever mine eyes desired I kept not from them, I withheld not my heart from any joy; for my heart rejoiced in all my labour: and this was my portion of all my labour. [11] Then I looked on all the works that my hands had wrought, and on the labour that I had laboured to do: and, behold, all was vanity and vexation of spirit, and there was no profit under the sun."
(Eccl. 2:10-11)

Non-believers.

Many people with great riches usually do not accept Jesus as Lord and Saviour. Therefore, they can't have joy. As a matter of fact, it seems to be the opposite (sadness) in their lives. This is because joy has not been promised to them. They think that joy can been derived from worldly pleasures. Sadly, they are confused.

The word of God teaches you that joy is only for God's children. Those that have been justified in the eyes of God.

"It is joy to the just to do judgment: but destruction shall be to the workers of iniquity." *(Prov. 21:15)*

"And they worshipped him, and returned to Jerusalem with great joy: [53] And were continually in the temple, praising and blessing God. Amen." *(Luke 24:52-53)*

Solomon could not find joy in the lust of his eyes

"And whatsoever mine eyes desired I kept not from them, I withheld not my heart from any joy; for my heart rejoiced in all my labour: and this was my portion of all my labour. [11] Then I looked on all the works that my hands had wrought, and on the labour that I had laboured to do: and, behold, all was vanity and vexation of spirit, and there was no profit under the sun." *(Eccl. 2:10-11)*

Silliness is considered joy to a fool.

"Folly is joy to him that is destitute of wisdom: but a man of understanding walketh uprightly." *(Prov. 15:21)*

To the children of Israel in the return to their land of promise.

"And the ransomed of the Lord shall return, and come to Zion with songs and everlasting joy upon their heads: they shall obtain joy and gladness, and sorrow and sighing shall flee away." *(Is. 35:10)*

"For ye shall go out with joy, and be led forth with peace: the mountains and the hills shall break forth before you into singing, and all the trees of the field shall clap their hands." *(Is. 55:12)*

Don't forget the joy that will be radiating in the lives of the saints in the future worship of the King of Kings in Jerusalem.

"Even them will I bring to my holy mountain, and make them joyful in my house of prayer: their burnt offerings and their sacrifices shall be accepted upon mine altar; for mine house shall be called an house of prayer for all people." *(Is. 56:7)* See additional references. Is. 2:2-4; Zech. 14:16-21

"Whom having not seen, ye love; in whom, though now ye see him not, yet believing, ye rejoice with joy unspeakable and full of glory."
(1 Pet. 1:8)

For all the children of God - Money can't buy this type of blessing. However, if you learn how to delight yourself in the Lord and wait on Him, He will bless you with your true inheritance.

All Believers should live in joy.

What about the joy in the early church.

"And they continued stedfastly in the apostles' doctrine and fellowship, and in breaking of bread, and in prayers. [43] And fear came upon every soul: and many wonders and signs were done by the apostles. [44] And all that believed were together, and had all things common; [45] And sold their possessions and goods, and parted them to all men, as every man had need. [46] And they, continuing daily with one accord in the temple, and breaking bread from house to house, did eat their meat with gladness and singleness of heart, [47] Praising God, and having favour with all the people. And the Lord added to the church daily such as should be saved."
(Acts 2:42-47)

See additional references. Acts 8:8, 13:52, 15:3

THINGS MONEY CAN'T BUY

Unlike the world, saints can be joyful even in the midst of afflictions.

"And to him they agreed: and when they had called the apostles, and beaten them, they commanded that they should not speak in the name of Jesus, and let them go. [41] And they departed from the presence of the council, rejoicing that they were counted worthy to suffer shame for his name. [42] And daily in the temple, and in every house, they ceased not to teach and preach Jesus Christ." *(Acts 5:40-42)*

"But call to remembrance the former days, in which, after ye were illuminated, ye endured a great fight of afflictions; [33] Partly, whilst ye were made a gazingstock both by reproaches and afflictions; and partly, whilst ye became companions of them that were so used. [34] For ye had compassion of me in my bonds, and took joyfully the spoiling of your goods, knowing in yourselves that ye have in heaven a better and an enduring substance." *(Heb. 10:32-34)*

"James, a servant of God and of the Lord Jesus Christ, to the twelve tribes which are scattered abroad, greeting. [2] My brethren, count it all joy when ye fall into divers temptations; [3] Knowing this, that the trying of your faith worketh patience." *(James 1:1-3)*

Joy is one of the blessings of being in the kingdom of God. If you are in the kingdom of God, rejoice in your joy, in the Holy Ghost.

"And not only so, but we also joy in God through our Lord Jesus Christ, by whom we have now received the atonement." *(Rom. 5:11)*

See additional references. Gal. 5:22; 1 Pet. 1:8

"If the Lord delight in us, then he will bring us into this land, and give it us; a land which floweth with milk and honey." *(Num. 14:8)*

"That the triumphing of the wicked is short, and the joy of the hypocrite but for a moment." *(Job 20:5)*

JOY

Joy is not for the wicked. This is why you see worldly people living a roller coaster life. One day they are up, and the next day, they are down. Their perception on life is based upon what is externally happening around them. A saint's outlook on life is based upon what is on the inside. Christ in you, the hope of glory.

David knew where joy could be found

"Thou wilt shew me the path of life: in thy presence is fulness of joy; at thy right hand there are pleasures for evermore." *(Ps. 16:11)*

"There be many that say, Who will shew us any good? Lord, lift thou up the light of thy countenance upon us. [7] Thou hast put gladness in my heart, more than in the time that their corn and their wine increased."
(Ps. 4:6-7) See also. Ps. 43:4

Solomon had to learn where joy could be found

"For God giveth to a man that is good in his sight wisdom, and knowledge, and joy: but to the sinner he giveth travail, to gather and to heap up, that he may give to him that is good before God. This also is vanity and vexation of spirit." *(Eccl. 2:26)*

One of the reasons for Christ coming was to anoint with the spirit of joy.

"To appoint unto them that mourn in Zion, to give unto them beauty for ashes, the oil of joy for mourning, the garment of praise for the spirit of heaviness; that they might be called trees of righteousness, the planting of the Lord, that he might be glorified." *(Is. 61:3)*

Another name for joy is the oil of gladness.

"Thou lovest righteousness, and hatest wickedness: therefore God, thy God, hath anointed thee with the oil of gladness above thy fellows."
(Ps. 45:7)

Always remember. The joy of the Lord is your strength.

"Then he said unto them, Go your way, eat the fat, and drink the sweet, and send portions unto them for whom nothing is prepared: for this day is holy unto our Lord: neither be ye sorry; for the joy of the Lord is your strength." *(Neh. 8:10)*

As a saint of God, it is the joy of Jesus that especially helps you through the tough times in life.

In times of sorrow

"And the ransomed of the Lord shall return, and come to Zion with songs and everlasting joy upon their heads: they shall obtain joy and gladness, and sorrow and sighing shall flee away." *(Is. 35:10)*

"As sorrowful, yet alway rejoicing; as poor, yet making many rich; as having nothing, and yet possessing all things." *(2 Cor. 6:10)*

In times of afflictions

"Verily, verily, I say unto you, That ye shall weep and lament, but the world shall rejoice: and ye shall be sorrowful, but your sorrow shall be turned into joy." *(John 16:20)*

"Behold, the hour cometh, yea, is now come, that ye shall be scattered, every man to his own, and shall leave me alone: and yet I am not alone, because the Father is with me. [33] These things I have spoken unto you, that in me ye might have peace. In the world ye shall have tribulation: but be of good cheer; I have overcome the world." *(John 16:32-33)*

"For his anger endureth but a moment; in his favour is life: weeping may endure for a night, but joy cometh in the morning." *(Ps. 30:5)*

"They that sow in tears shall reap in joy." *(Ps. 126:5)*

Times in spiritual court

"My brethren, count it all joy when ye fall into divers temptations."
(James 1:2)

"Wherein ye greatly rejoice, though now for a season, if need be, ye are in heaviness through manifold temptations." *(1 Pet. 1:6)*

Times of Persecutions

"Blessed are ye, when men shall hate you, and when they shall separate you from their company, and shall reproach you, and cast out your name as evil, for the Son of man's sake. [23] Rejoice ye in that day, and leap for joy: for, behold, your reward is great in heaven: for in the like manner did their fathers unto the prophets." *(Luke 6:22-23)*

"Blessed are ye, when men shall revile you, and persecute you, and shall say all manner of evil against you falsely, for my sake. [12] Rejoice, and be exceeding glad: for great is your reward in heaven: for so persecuted they the prophets which were before you. [13] Ye are the salt of the earth: but if the salt have lost his savour, wherewith shall it be salted? it is thenceforth good for nothing, but to be cast out, and to be trodden under foot of men." *(Matt. 5:11-13)*

"Partly, whilst ye were made a gazingstock both by reproaches and afflictions; and partly, whilst ye became companions of them that were so used. [34] For ye had compassion of me in my bonds, and took joyfully the spoiling of your goods, knowing in yourselves that ye have in heaven a better and an enduring substance." *(Heb. 10:33-34)*

Times of famine

"Although the fig tree shall not blossom, neither shall fruit be in the vines; the labour of the olive shall fail, and the fields shall yield no meat; the flock shall be cut off from the fold, and there shall be no herd in the stalls: [18] Yet I will rejoice in the Lord, I will joy in the God of my salvation."
(Hab. 3:17-18)

"For if, when we were enemies, we were reconciled to God by the death of his Son, much more, being reconciled, we shall be saved by his life. [11] And not only so, but we also joy in God through our Lord Jesus Christ, by whom we have now received the atonement." *(Rom. 5:10-11)*

Joy can even be brought to you in the form of an angel.

The birth of Jesus to all mankind

"And, lo, the angel of the Lord came upon them, and the glory of the Lord shone round about them: and they were sore afraid. [10] And the angel said unto them, Fear not: for, behold, I bring you good tidings of great joy, which shall be to all people." *(Luke 2:9-10)*

Continuous and full joy in the presence of God

"Rejoice in the Lord alway: and again I say, Rejoice." *(Phil. 4:4)*

"Looking unto Jesus the author and finisher of our faith; who for the joy that was set before him endured the cross, despising the shame, and is set down at the right hand of the throne of God." *(Heb. 12:2)*

The joy of the Lord can only be found in His salvation

"And my soul shall be joyful in the Lord: it shall rejoice in his salvation." *(Ps. 35:9)*   See also. Hab. 3:18

What about happiness ?

"Happy is that people, that is in such a case: yea, happy is that people, whose God is the Lord." *(Ps. 144:15)*

See other references on happiness. Job 5:17; Ps. 146:5; Prov. 3:13-15, 16:20, 28:14, 29:18; 1 Kgs. 10:8; 2 Chr. 9:7; John 13:17; 1 Pet. 3:14,4:14

CHAPTER 12

PEACE (a state of wholeness)

The brother of Jesus said this about God

"But if ye have bitter envying and strife in your hearts, glory not, and lie not against the truth. [15] This wisdom descendeth not from above, but is earthly, sensual, devilish. [16] For where envying and strife is, there is confusion and every evil work. [17] But the wisdom that is from above is first pure, then peaceable, gentle, and easy to be intreated, full of mercy and good fruits, without partiality, and without hypocrisy." *(James 3:14-17)*

Paul's words concerning peace

"For God is not the author of confusion, but of peace, as in all churches of the saints." *(1 Cor. 14:33)*

The word peace comes from the Hebrew word Shalown "Shaw-lome". It simply means well, happy, friendly, good health, prosperity, favor, rest, safety and wholeness.

It comes from the Greek word Eirene "I-ray-nay". It means a state of rest, contentment or wholeness.

Peace comes from the gospel

"Then Gideon built an altar there unto the Lord, and called it Jehovah-shalom: unto this day it is yet in Ophrah of the Abi-ezrites." *(Judg. 6:24)*

"And how shall they preach, except they be sent? as it is written, How beautiful are the feet of them that preach the gospel of peace, and bring good tidings of good things." *(Rom. 10:15)*   See also. Prov. 3:1-2; Is. 48:18

"I will both lay me down in peace, and sleep: for thou, Lord, only makest me dwell in safety." *(Ps. 4:8)*

"The Lord will give strength unto his people; the Lord will bless his people with peace." *(Ps. 29:11)*

"Lord, thou wilt ordain peace for us: for thou also hast wrought all our works in us. [13] O Lord our God, other lords besides thee have had dominion over us: but by thee only will we make mention of thy name. [14] They are dead, they shall not live; they are deceased, they shall not rise: therefore hast thou visited and destroyed them, and made all their memory to perish." *(Is. 26:12-14)*

"Behold, I will bring it health and cure, and I will cure them, and will reveal unto them the abundance of peace and truth." *(Jer. 33:6)*

Only God can bring peace to your situation. He loves you so - that He created a covenant of peace for all His children.

"And the Lord spake unto Moses, saying, [11] Phinehas, the son of Eleazar, the son of Aaron the priest, hath turned my wrath away from the children of Israel, while he was zealous for my sake among them, that I consumed not the children of Israel in my jealousy. [12] Wherefore say, Behold, I give unto him my covenant of peace: [13] And he shall have it, and his seed after him, even the covenant of an everlasting priesthood; because he was zealous for his God, and made an atonement for the children of Israel."
(Num. 25:10-13)   See also. Gal. 3:26-29

The Jews and Gentiles make up the
New Testament church

"Of whom the whole family in heaven and earth is named." *(Eph. 3:15)*

"The secret of the Lord is with them that fear him; and he will shew them his covenant." *(Ps. 25:14)*

"His soul shall dwell at ease; and his seed shall inherit the earth."
(Ps. 25:13)

It was through the atoning work of Christ, that the children of God can live with a peace of mind, regardless of what is going on around them.

"Surely he hath borne our griefs, and carried our sorrows: yet we did esteem him stricken, smitten of God, and afflicted. [5] But he was wounded for our transgressions, he was bruised for our iniquities: the chastisement of our peace was upon him; and with his stripes we are healed." *(Is. 53:4-5)*

God's promise to never abandon the covenant of peace for His children

"For the mountains shall depart, and the hills be removed; but my kindness shall not depart from thee, neither shall the covenant of my peace be removed, saith the Lord that hath mercy on thee." *(Is. 54:10)*

Jesus will make a covenant of peace with Israel at His second coming

"And I will make with them a covenant of peace, and will cause the evil beasts to cease out of the land: and they shall dwell safely in the wilderness, and sleep in the woods." *(Ezek. 34:25)*

"For he is our peace, who hath made both one, and hath broken down the middle wall of partition between us; [15] Having abolished in his flesh the enmity, even the law of commandments contained in ordinances; for to make in himself of twain one new man, so making peace." *(Eph. 2:14,15)*

"And, having made peace through the blood of his cross, by him to reconcile all things unto himself; by him, I say, whether they be things in earth, or things in heaven." *(Col. 1:20)*

"Now the Lord of peace himself give you peace always by all means. The Lord be with you all." *(2 Thess. 3:16)*

"And thou, child, shalt be called the prophet of the Highest: for thou shalt go before the face of the Lord to prepare his ways; [77] To give knowledge of salvation unto his people by the remission of their sins, [78] Through the tender mercy of our God; whereby the dayspring from on high hath visited us, [79] To give light to them that sit in darkness and in the shadow of death, to guide our feet into the way of peace."
(Luke 1:76-79)

See additional references. Heb. 13:20; Eccl. 5:12; John 14:27; Ps. 23:2; Ps. 29:11

Peace is only for the righteous. (even perfect peace)

"In that day shall this song be sung in the land of Judah; We have a strong city; salvation will God appoint for walls and bulwarks. [2] Open ye the gates, that the righteous nation which keepeth the truth may enter in. [3] Thou wilt keep him in perfect peace, whose mind is stayed on thee: because he trusteth in thee. [4] Trust ye in the Lord for ever: for in the Lord Jehovah is everlasting strength." *(Is. 26:1-4)*

Peace is a fruit of the Spirit

"For the kingdom of God is not meat and drink; but righteousness, and peace, and joy in the Holy Ghost." *(Rom. 14:17)*

"But the fruit of the Spirit is love, joy, peace, longsuffering, gentleness, goodness, faith, [23] Meekness, temperance: against such there is no law." *(Gal. 5:22-23)*

Peace is not for the wicked

"There is no peace, saith the Lord, unto the wicked." *(Is. 48:22)*

"But the wicked are like the troubled sea, when it cannot rest, whose waters cast up mire and dirt. [21] There is no peace, saith my God, to the wicked." *(Is. 57:20-21)*

"As it is written, There is none righteous, no, not one: [11] There is none that understandeth, there is none that seeketh after God. [12] They are all gone out of the way, they are together become unprofitable; there is none that doeth good, no, not one. [13] Their throat is an open sepulchre; with their tongues they have used deceit; the poison of asps is under their lips: [14] Whose mouth is full of cursing and bitterness: [15] Their feet are swift to shed blood: [16] Destruction and misery are in their ways: [17] And the way of peace have they not known." *(Rom. 3:10-17)*

Peace between God and man
Acts 10:36; Eph. 2:17

1. You must make <u>peace with God</u> by being born again. Rom. 5:1; John 16:33; Job 22:21(NIV)

   Peace is even for your children, through the word of God. Is. 54:13

2. Experience the <u>peace of God</u> in every area of your life by abiding in God. Col. 3:15-16; Phil. 4:7; Ps. 119:165 (Great Peace - Complete safety and well-being in God); Is. 32:17 (By working the righteousness of God)

Peace between man and man
Rom. 12:18, 14:19; 2 Tim. 2:22; 2 Cor. 13:11; Eph. 4:3; Heb. 12:14

Peace between nation and nation
Acts 12:18-24; Rev. 6:4

What about world peace ?

The apostle Paul had this to say about your fight against the enemy

"For we wrestle not against flesh and blood, but against principalities, against powers, against the rulers of the darkness of this world, against spiritual wickedness in high places." *(Eph. 6:12)*

Peace can't be purchased with money. Money can only buy a degree of stability.

Billions of dollars are spent each year around the world on trying to secure peace. But as a child of God, we know that there will be no world peace until this world is renovated by fire and Jesus is crowned King of Kings and Lord of Lords here on earth. As a child of God, you are in this world but not of the world. Therefore, it does not matter what is happening in the world.

God desires peace between nation and nation

During the time of Peter, Herod was an enemy of Peter. God allowed him to be removed from office so that the gospel of peace could be preached.

"Now as soon as it was day, there was no small stir among the soldiers, what was become of Peter. [19] And when Herod had sought for him, and found him not, he examined the keepers, and commanded that they should be put to death. And he went down from Judaea to Caesarea, and there abode. [20] And Herod was highly displeased with them of Tyre and Sidon: but they came with one accord to him, and, having made Blastus the king's chamberlain their friend, desired peace; because their country was nourished by the king's country. [21] And upon a set day Herod, arrayed in royal apparel, sat upon his throne, and made an oration unto them. [22] And the people gave a shout, saying, It is the voice of a god, and not of a man. [23] And immediately the angel of the Lord smote him, because he gave not God the glory: and he was eaten of worms, and gave up the ghost. [24] But the word of God grew and multiplied." *(Acts 12:18-24)*

The prophet Isaiah prophesied that there would be one called the Prince of Peace.

"For unto us a child is born, unto us a son is given: and the government shall be upon his shoulder: and his name shall be called Wonderful, Counsellor, The mighty God, The everlasting Father, The Prince of Peace. [7] Of the increase of his government and peace there shall be no end, upon the throne of David, and upon his kingdom, to order it, and to establish it with judgment and with justice from henceforth even for ever. The zeal of the Lord of hosts will perform this." *(Is. 9:6-7)*

Future world peace

"The word that Isaiah the son of Amoz saw concerning Judah and Jerusalem. [2] And it shall come to pass in the last days, that the mountain of the Lord's house shall be established in the top of the mountains, and shall be exalted above the hills; and all nations shall flow unto it. [3] And many people shall go and say, Come ye, and let us go up to the mountain of the Lord, to the house of the God of Jacob; and he will teach us of his ways, and we will walk in his paths: for out of Zion shall go forth the law, and the word of the Lord from Jerusalem. [4] And he shall judge among the nations, and shall rebuke many people: and they shall beat their swords into plowshares, and their spears into pruninghooks: nation shall not lift up sword against nation, neither shall they learn war any more." *(Is. 2:1-4)*

See additional references. Is. 32:18; Jer. 8:10, 31:34; Heb. 8:11

You should never stop praying for the peace of Jerusalem. God said of those that bless Israel, they shall be blessed.

"Pray for the peace of Jerusalem: they shall prosper that love thee."
(Ps. 122:6)

Peace shall one day be upon Israel.

"As for such as turn aside unto their crooked ways, the Lord shall lead them forth with the workers of iniquity: but peace shall be upon Israel."
(Ps. 125:5)

Beware of the prophesies of false peace

"Then said I, Ah, Lord God! behold, the prophets say unto them, Ye shall not see the sword, neither shall ye have famine; but I will give you assured peace in this place. [14] Then the Lord said unto me, The prophets prophesy lies in my name: I sent them not, neither have I commanded them, neither spake unto them: they prophesy unto you a false vision and divination, and a thing of nought, and the deceit of their heart."
(Jer. 14:13-14)

PEACE

**A peaceful home is more important than just a
material prosperous home**

"Better is a dinner of herbs where love is, than a stalled ox and hatred therewith." *(Prov. 15:17)*

"Better is a dry morsel, and quietness therewith, than an house full of sacrifices with strife." *(Prov. 17:1)*

"But godliness with contentment is great gain." *(1 Tim. 6:6)*

CHAPTER 13

CONTENTMENT (state of satisfaction)

"But godliness with contentment is great gain. [7] For we brought nothing into this world, and it is certain we can carry nothing out. [8] And having food and raiment let us be therewith content." *(1 Tim. 6:6-8)*

"A little that a righteous man hath is better than the riches of many wicked." *(Ps. 37:16)*

"The righteous eateth to the satisfying of his soul: but the belly of the wicked shall want." *(Prov. 13:25)*

See additional references. Prov. 3:5-6,15:16, 16:8; 1 Thess. 5:18

"My flesh and my heart faileth: but God is the strength of my heart, and my portion for ever." *(Ps. 73:26)*

"I cried unto thee, O Lord: I said, Thou art my refuge and my portion in the land of the living. [6] Attend unto my cry; for I am brought very low: deliver me from my persecutors; for they are stronger than I. [7] Bring my soul out of prison, that I may praise thy name: the righteous shall compass me about; for thou shalt deal bountifully with me." *(Ps. 142:5-7)*

Once you learn to accept Jesus as your daily portion, you will have no problem with contentment. David found this to be true.

"I cried unto thee, O Lord: I said, Thou art my refuge and my portion in the land of the living." *(Ps. 142:5)*

CONTENTMENT

God's encouraging words to Joshua

"There shall not any man be able to stand before thee all the days of thy life: as I was with Moses, so I will be with thee: I will not fail thee, nor forsake thee." *(Josh. 1:5)*

David's encouraging words to his son Solomon

"And David said to Solomon his son, Be strong and of good courage, and do it: fear not, nor be dismayed: for the Lord God, even my God, will be with thee; he will not fail thee, nor forsake thee, until thou hast finished all the work for the service of the house of the Lord." *(1 Chr. 28:20)*

Paul's exhortation to the Hebrews

"Keep your lives free from the love of money and be content with what you have, because God has said, Never will I leave you; never will I forsake you." *(Heb. 13:5 NIV)*

"For in him we live, and move, and have our being; as certain also of your own poets have said, For we are also his offspring. [29] Forasmuch then as we are the offspring of God, we ought not to think that the Godhead is like unto gold, or silver, or stone, graven by art and man's device."
(Acts 17:28-29)

"Wait on the Lord, and keep his way, and he shall exalt thee to inherit the land: when the wicked are cut off, thou shalt see it." *(Ps. 37:4-5)*

"As for me, I will behold thy face in righteousness: I shall be satisfied, when I awake, with thy likeness." *(Ps. 17:15)*

Although the wicked desires contentment, it is not for them.

"He that loveth silver shall not be satisfied with silver; nor he that loveth abundance with increase: this is also vanity." *(Eccl. 5:10)*

Learn how to trust and wait on God

"For the Lord God is a sun and shield: the Lord will give grace and glory: no good thing will he withhold from them that walk uprightly." *(Ps. 84:11)*

"And God is able to make all grace abound toward you; that ye, always having all sufficiency in all things, may abound to every good work." *(2 Cor. 9:8)*

You are to reach that state of contentment as Paul did. He was able to be satisfied in any situation.

"Not that I speak in respect of want: for I have learned, in whatsoever state I am, therewith to be content. [12] I know both how to be abased, and I know how to abound: every where and in all things I am instructed both to be full and to be hungry, both to abound and to suffer need." *(Phil. 4:11-12)*

CHAPTER 14

LIBERTY (freedom)

Paul's preaching to the Romans about true liberty

"For the creature was made subject to vanity, not willingly, but by reason of him who hath subjected the same in hope, [21] Because the creature itself also shall be delivered from the bondage of corruption into the glorious liberty of the children of God. [22] For we know that the whole creation groaneth and travaileth in pain together until now. " *(Rom. 8:20-22)*

"If the Son therefore shall make you free, ye shall be free indeed."
(2 Cor. 3:17)

"Stand fast therefore in the liberty wherewith Christ hath made us free, and be not entangled again with the yoke of bondage." *(Gal. 5:1)*

True liberty can only be found in God

"Tell me, ye that desire to be under the law, do ye not hear the law? [22] For it is written, that Abraham had two sons, the one by a bondmaid, the other by a freewoman. [23] But he who was of the bondwoman was born after the flesh; but he of the freewoman was by promise. [24] Which things are an allegory: for these are the two covenants; the one from the mount Sinai, which gendereth to bondage, which is Agar. [25] For this Agar is mount Sinai in Arabia, and answereth to Jerusalem which now is, and is in bondage with her children. [26] But Jerusalem which is above is free, which is the mother of us all. [27] For it is written, Rejoice, thou barren that bearest not; break forth and cry, thou that travailest not: for the desolate hath many more children than she which hath an husband. [28] Now we, brethren, as Isaac was, are the children of promise. [29] But as then he that was born after the flesh persecuted him that was born after the Spirit, even so it is now. [30] Nevertheless what saith the scripture? Cast out the bondwoman and her son: for the son of the bondwoman shall not be heir with the son of the free woman. [31] So then, brethren, we are not children of the bondwoman, but of the free." *(Gal. 4:21-31)*

"But whoso looketh into the perfect law of liberty, and continueth therein, he being not a forgetful hearer, but a doer of the work, this man shall be blessed in his deed." *(James 1:25)*

Money can't buy real freedom. Your liberty in God gives you all the freedom you need. Those who try to purchase liberty (freedom) with money and not inculde the most important factor (The **Prince of Peace - Jesus**) will always be disappointed with the results.

"Because the creature itself also shall be delivered from the bondage of corruption into the glorious liberty of the children of God." *(Rom. 8:21)*

Liberty can only be found in God. If anyone tries to convince you otherwise, flee from them. Jesus is the only one that can give you true liberty.

Beware of false prophets

"While they promise them liberty, they themselves are the servants of corruption: for of whom a man is overcome, of the same is he brought in bondage." *(2 Pet. 2:19)*

Through God the Father

"Giving thanks unto the Father, which hath made us meet to be partakers of the inheritance of the saints in light: [13] Who hath delivered us from the power of darkness, and hath translated us into the kingdom of his dear Son: [14] In whom we have redemption through his blood, even the forgiveness of sins." *(Col. 1:12-14)*

THINGS MONEY CAN'T BUY

Through His son Jesus

"The Spirit of the Lord is upon me, because he hath anointed me to preach the gospel to the poor; he hath sent me to heal the brokenhearted, to preach deliverance to the captives, and recovering of sight to the blind, to set at liberty them that are bruised." *(Luke 4:18)*

Through the Holy Spirit

"For ye have not received the spirit of bondage again to fear; but ye have received the Spirit of adoption, whereby we cry, Abba, Father." *(Rom. 8:15)*

"Now the Lord is that Spirit: and where the Spirit of the Lord is, there is liberty." *(2 Cor. 3:17)*

Through the word of God

"Then said Jesus to those Jews which believed on him, If ye continue in my word, then are ye my disciples indeed; [32] And ye shall know the truth, and the truth shall make you free." *(John 8:31-32)*

Liberty is not for the wicked

"Jesus answered them, Verily, verily, I say unto you, Whosoever committeth sin is the servant of sin." *(John 8:34)*

When you are born again by accepting the perfect sacrifice that Jesus paid for the redemption of man, you are delivered from such things as the following.

Curse of the law.

"Christ hath redeemed us from the curse of the law, being made a curse for us: for it is written, Cursed is every one that hangeth on a tree: [14] That the blessing of Abraham might come on the Gentiles through Jesus Christ; that we might receive the promise of the Spirit through faith." *(Gal. 3:13-14)*

Law.

"But now we are delivered from the law, that being dead wherein we were held; that we should serve in newness of spirit, and not in the oldness of the letter." *(Rom. 7:6)*

"For the law of the Spirit of life in Christ Jesus hath made me free from the law of sin and death." *(Rom. 8:2)*

Bondage of man.

"What is my reward then? Verily that, when I preach the gospel, I may make the gospel of Christ without charge, that I abuse not my power in the gospel. [19] For though I be free from all men, yet have I made myself servant unto all, that I might gain the more." *(1 Cor. 9:18-19)*

Slave to sin.

"Knowing this, that our old man is crucified with him, that the body of sin might be destroyed, that henceforth we should not serve sin. [7] For he that is dead is freed from sin. [17] But God be thanked, that ye were the servants of sin, but ye have obeyed from the heart that form of doctrine which was delivered you. [18] Being then made free from sin, ye became the servants of righteousness." *(Rom. 6:6-7,17,18)*

"For he hath made him to be sin for us, who knew no sin;
that we might be made the righteousness of God in him." *(2 Cor. 5:21)*

CHAPTER 15

FORGIVENESS OF SIN

Your works nor your money can qualify for the ransom price of the forgiveness of sin. God knew what was necessary to pay the price. He sent His Son Jesus. Jesus was the propitiation (true atonement) for your sins. In a simpler term, Jesus became your substitute.

"Being justified freely by his grace through the redemption that is in Christ Jesus: [25] Whom God hath set forth to be a propitiation through faith in his blood, to declare his righteousness for the remission of sins that are past, through the forbearance of God." *(Rom. 3:24-25)*

"And he is the propitiation for our sins: and not for ours only, but also for the sins of the whole world." *(1 John 2:2)*

"And we have seen and do testify that the Father sent the Son to be the Saviour of the world." *(1 John 4:14)*

"For ye are bought with a price: therefore glorify God in your body, and in your spirit, which are God's." *(1 Cor. 6:20)*

"For God so loved the world, that he gave his only begotten Son, that whosoever believeth in him should not perish, but have everlasting life." *(John 3:16)*

"To open their eyes, and to turn them from darkness to light, and from the power of Satan unto God, that they may receive forgiveness of sins, and inheritance among them which are sanctified by faith that is in me." *(Acts 26:18)*

"In whom we have redemption through his blood, the forgiveness of sins, according to the riches of his grace." *(Eph. 1:7)*

"Wherefore in all things it behoved him to be made like unto his brethren, that he might be a merciful and faithful high priest in things pertaining to God, to make reconciliation for the sins of the people." *(Heb. 2:17)*

The blood of Jesus cleanses you from all sins

"If we confess our sins, he is faithful and just to forgive us our sins, and to cleanse us from all unrighteousness." *(1 John 1:9)*   See also Matt. 26:28

The blood of Jesus continues to cleanse you from all sin as you obey His word.

"But if we walk in the light, as he is in the light, we have fellowship one with another, and the blood of Jesus Christ his Son cleanseth us from all sin." *(1 John 1:7)*

This is what you must do to receive the forgiveness of sin

"Repent ye therefore, and be converted, that your sins may be blotted out, when the times of refreshing shall come from the presence of the Lord." *(Acts 3:19)*

See additional references. Acts 2:21; 17:29-30; Ps. 19:7, 51:13; Matt. 18:1-3; Eph. 1:7; Luke 13:3; Rom. 10:9-10.

CHAPTER 16

REST (stillness-calmness)

You should be concern with two basic types of rest.

1. Present rest. This can only be found in Christ.
"I sought the Lord, and he heard me, and delivered me from all my fears."
(Ps. 34:4)

"Come unto me, all ye that labour and are heavy laden, and I will give you
rest. [29] Take my yoke upon you, and learn of me; for I am meek and lowly
in heart: and ye shall find rest unto your souls. [30] For my yoke is easy,
and my burden is light." *(Matt. 11:28-30)*

"For we which have believed do enter into rest, as he said, As I have sworn
in my wrath, if they shall enter into my rest: although the works were finished from the foundation of the world." *(Heb. 4:3)*

In your storms of life.

"And when they had sent away the multitude, they took him even as he was
in the ship. And there were also with him other little ships. [37] And there
arose a great storm of wind, and the waves beat into the ship, so that it was
now full. [38] And he was in the hinder part of the ship, asleep on a pillow:
and they awake him, and say unto him, Master, carest thou not that we perish? [39] And he arose, and rebuked the wind, and said unto the sea,
Peace, be still. And the wind ceased, and there was a great calm."
(Mark 4:36-39)

"Behold, he that keepeth Israel shall neither slumber nor sleep."
(Ps. 121:4)

"It is vain for you to rise up early, to sit up late, to eat the bread of sorrows: for so he giveth his beloved sleep." *(Ps. 127:2)*

"When thou liest down, thou shalt not be afraid: yea, thou shalt lie down, and thy sleep shall be sweet." *(Prov. 3:24)*

"The sleep of a labouring man is sweet, whether he eat little or much: but the abundance of the rich will not suffer him to sleep." *(Eccl. 5:12)*

2. Eternal rest. Your future life with God.

"Wherefore I was grieved with that generation, and said, They do alway err in their heart; and they have not known my ways. [11] So I sware in my wrath, They shall not enter into my rest.) [12] Take heed, brethren, lest there be in any of you an evil heart of unbelief, in departing from the living God. [13] But exhort one another daily, while it is called To day; lest any of you be hardened through the deceitfulness of sin. [14] For we are made partakers of Christ, if we hold the beginning of our confidence stedfast unto the end." *(Heb. 3:10-14)*   See also. Is. 57:1-2; Phil. 1:21,22

This rest is only for the righteous.

"And I heard a voice from heaven saying unto me, Write, Blessed are the dead which die in the Lord from henceforth: Yea, saith the Spirit, that they may rest from their labours; and their works do follow them." *(Rev. 14:13)*

There will be no rest for the wicked.

"And the smoke of their torment ascendeth up for ever and ever: and they have no rest day nor night, who worship the beast and his image, and whosoever receiveth the mark of his name." *(Rev. 14:11)*

Rest can only be found in God - The true and living God, not any of the false dead gods.

"Rest in the Lord, and wait patiently for him: fret not thyself because of him who prospereth in his way, because of the man who bringeth wicked devices to pass." *(Ps. 37:7)*   See also. Ps. 62:5

"There is no soundness in my flesh because of thine anger; neither is there any rest in my bones because of my sin." *(Ps. 38:3)*

"But the wicked are like the troubled sea, when it cannot rest, whose waters cast up mire and dirt. [21] There is no peace, saith my God, to the wicked." *(Is. 57:20-21)*

Rest is not to be found for those that disobey the word of God.

"Forty years long was I grieved with this generation, and said, It is a people that do err in their heart, and they have not known my ways: [11] Unto whom I sware in my wrath that they should not enter into my rest." *(Ps. 95:10-11)*

The rest in the communication with God in His own language, the gift of tongues.

"For with stammering lips and another tongue will he speak to this people. [12] To whom he said, This is the rest wherewith ye may cause the weary to rest; and this is the refreshing: yet they would not hear." *(Is. 28:11-12)*

"Thus saith the Lord, Stand ye in the ways, and see, and ask for the old paths, where is the good way, and walk therein, and ye shall find rest for your souls. But they said, We will not walk therein." *(Jer. 6:16)*

"Their Redeemer is strong; the Lord of hosts is his name: he shall throughly plead their cause, that he may give rest to the land, and disquiet the inhabitants of Babylon." *(Jer. 50:34)*

The reason why most people are restless is simple because they have not accepted Jesus as Lord and Saviour. When this happens, everyday is a day of rest. Because it is in Him that we live, move and have our being. See Hebrews 4:1-11 for attaining true rest (spiritual sabbath) by faith in God.

True rest is only for the children of God

"There remaineth therefore a rest to the people of God." *(Heb. 4:9)*

Remember, you can only experience true rest by having the Spirit of the Lord

"Then he remembered the days of old, Moses, and his people, saying, Where is he that brought them up out of the sea with the shepherd of his flock? where is he that put his holy Spirit within him? [12] That led them by the right hand of Moses with his glorious arm, dividing the water before them, to make himself an everlasting name? [13] That led them through the deep, as an horse in the wilderness, that they should not stumble? [14] As a beast goeth down into the valley, the Spirit of the Lord caused him to rest: so didst thou lead thy people, to make thyself a glorious name."
(Is. 63:11-14)

CHAPTER 17

REAL MAN OF GOD

Let the word of God speak to you.

"Ye are bought with a price; be not ye the servants of men. [24] Brethren, let every man, wherein he is called, therein abide with God." *(1 Cor. 7:23-24)*

"Paul, an apostle of Jesus Christ by the commandment of God our Saviour, and Lord Jesus Christ, which is our hope; [2] Unto Timothy, my own son in the faith: Grace, mercy, and peace, from God our Father and Jesus Christ our Lord." *(1 Tim. 1:1-2)*

"Now there were in the church that was at Antioch certain prophets and teachers; as Barnabas, and Simeon that was called Niger, and Lucius of Cyrene, and Manaen, which had been brought up with Herod the tetrarch, and Saul. [2] As they ministered to the Lord, and fasted, the Holy Ghost said, Separate me Barnabas and Saul for the work whereunto I have called them. [3] And when they had fasted and prayed, and laid their hands on them, they sent them away." *(Acts 13:1-3)*

"And God hath set some in the church, first apostles, secondarily prophets, thirdly teachers, after that miracles, then gifts of healings, helps, governments, diversities of tongues." *(1 Cor. 12:28)*

"For the gifts and calling of God are without repentance." *(Rom. 11:29)*

REAL MAN OF GOD

Let us look at a few of God's elect who could not be bought with riches.

1. Abraham. His father's wealth could not stop him from obeying God.
   Gen. 12:1,14:; Josh. 24:2; Gen. 14:21-23 king of Sodom
2. Moses.   Heb. 11:24-27
3. Job. Job 1:21
4. Daniel.   Dan. 1:8, 5:13-17
5. Jesus. Matt. 4:1-11. He turned down all the kingdoms of this world.
   Jesus made it perfectly clear - You must live by every word of God.

One who turned out to be a wolf in sheep clothing. Judas was bought for thirty pieces of silver (Matt. 26:14-16). He thought he could sell the Son of God.

One who esteemed money more than the Messiah.

Ananias proved to God what his relationship was with money. Acts 5:1-11

Real promotions come from God

"Humble yourselves therefore under the mighty hand of God, that he may exalt you in due time." *(1 Pet. 5:6)*

The Lord will prosper you

"The Lord recompense thy work, and a full reward be given thee of the Lord God of Israel, under whose wings thou art come to trust."
(Ruth 2:12)

"Wealth gotten by vanity shall be diminished: but he that gathereth by labour shall increase." *(Prov. 13:11)*

"Be ye strong therefore, and let not your hands be weak: for your work shall be rewarded." *(2 Chr. 15:7)*

"The blessing of the Lord it maketh rich, and he added no sorrow with it." *(Prov. 10:22)*

THINGS MONEY CAN'T BUY

A hireling (one who works for pay only) can be bought

"As a servant earnestly desireth the shadow, and as an hireling looketh for the reward of his work." *(Job 7:2)*

"But he that is an hireling, and not the shepherd, whose own the sheep are not, seeth the wolf coming, and leaveth the sheep, and fleeth: and the wolf catcheth them, and scattereth the sheep. [13] The hireling fleeth, because he is an hireling, and careth not for the sheep." *(John 10:12-13)*

"But ye shall be named the Priests of the Lord: men shall call you the Ministers of our God: ye shall eat the riches of the Gentiles, and in their glory shall ye boast yourselves." *(Is. 61:6)*

David's priority of money

"The law of thy mouth is better unto me than thousands of gold and silver." *(Ps. 119:72)*

"Therefore I love thy commandments above gold; yea, above fine gold. [128] Therefore I esteem all thy precepts concerning all things to be right; and I hate every false way." *(Ps. 119:127-128)*

The story of the Man of God

"And the man of God said unto the king, If thou wilt give me half thine house, I will not go in with thee, neither will I eat bread nor drink water in this place." *(1 Kgs. 13:8)*

Read the entire story of 1 Kgs. 13:1-34.

CHAPTER 18

REAL WOMAN OF GOD

A real woman of God is one who esteems the value of Him and all that He stands for more than all the rubies in the world. This woman is a virtuous woman.

Now let us look at someone who knew a little about women. Solomon although not approved of God, had seven hundred wives and three hundred concubines and others.

"And he had seven hundred wives, princesses, and three hundred concubines: and his wives turned away his heart." *(1 Kgs. 11:3)*

Solomon asked the following question

"Who can find a virtuous woman? for her price is far above rubies." *(Prov. 31:10)*

Solomon below describes the quality of a virtuous woman

"Who can find a virtuous woman? for her price is far above rubies. [11] The heart of her husband doth safely trust in her, so that he shall have no need of spoil. [12] She will do him good and not evil all the days of her life. [13] She seeketh wool, and flax, and worketh willingly with her hands. [14] She is like the merchants' ships; she bringeth her food from afar. [15] She riseth also while it is yet night, and giveth meat to her household, and a portion to her maidens. [16] She considereth a field, and buyeth it: with the fruit of her hands she planteth a vineyard. [17] She girdeth her loins with strength, and strengtheneth her arms. [18] She perceiveth that her merchandise is good: her candle goeth not out by night. [19] She layeth her hands to the spindle, and her hands hold the distaff. [20] She stretcheth out her hand to the poor; yea, she reacheth forth her hands to the needy. [21] She is not afraid of the snow for her household: for all her household are clothed with scarlet. [22] She maketh herself coverings of tapestry; her clothing is silk and purple. [23] Her husband is known in the gates, when he sitteth among the elders of the land. [24] She maketh fine linen, and selleth it; and delivereth girdles unto the merchant. [25] Strength and honour are her clothing; and she shall rejoice in time to come. [26] She openeth her mouth with wisdom; and in her tongue is the law of kindness. [27] She looketh well to the ways of her household, and eateth not the bread of idleness. [28] Her children arise up, and call her blessed; her husband also, and he praiseth her. [29] Many daughters have done virtuously, but thou excellest them all. [30] Favour is deceitful, and beauty is vain: but a woman that feareth the Lord, she shall be praised. [31] Give her of the fruit of her hands; and let her own works praise her in the gates." *(Prov. 31:10-31)*

Ruth met the requirements of a virtuous woman.

Ruth's vow to righteousness

"And Ruth said, Intreat me not to leave thee, or to return from following after thee: for whither thou goest, I will go; and where thou lodgest, I will lodge: thy people shall be my people, and thy God my God." *(Ruth 1:16)*

"And he said, Blessed be thou of the Lord, my daughter: for thou hast shewed more kindness in the latter end than at the beginning, inasmuch as thou followedst not young men, whether poor or rich." *(Ruth 3:10)*

"And now, my daughter, fear not; I will do to thee all that thou requirest: for all the city of my people doth know that thou art a virtuous woman." *(Prov. 3:11)*

"A virtuous woman is a crown to her husband: but she that maketh ashamed is as rottenness in his bones." *(Prov. 12:4)*

Sapphira was a women who valued money more than she did the right-eousness of God. She allowed money to separate her from God. She did this by lying to God over rendering unto Him His financial sacrifices.

"But a certain man named Ananias, with Sapphira his wife, sold a posses-sion, [2] And kept back part of the price, his wife also being privy to it, and brought a certain part, and laid it at the apostles' feet. [3] But Peter said, Ananias, why hath Satan filled thine heart to lie to the Holy Ghost, and to keep back part of the price of the land? [4] Whiles it remained, was it not thine own? and after it was sold, was it not in thine own power? why hast thou conceived this thing in thine heart? thou hast not lied unto men, but unto God. [5] And Ananias hearing these words fell down, and gave up the ghost: and great fear came on all them that heard these things. [6] And the young men arose, wound him up, and carried him out, and buried him. [7] And it was about the space of three hours after, when his wife, not knowing what was done, came in. [8] And Peter answered unto her, Tell me whether ye sold the land for so much? And she said, Yea, for so much. [9] Then Peter said unto her, How is it that ye have agreed together to tempt the Spirit of the Lord? behold, the feet of them which have buried thy husband are at the door, and shall carry thee out. [10] Then fell she down straight-way at his feet, and yielded up the ghost: and the young men came in, and found her dead, and, carrying her forth, buried her by her husband. [11] And great fear came upon all the church, and upon as many as heard these things." *(Acts 5:1-11)*

You saw in the above reference that, not only did Sapphira allow money to be esteemed more than God. Her husband Ananias also yielded to the temptation of greed.

I often wonder at the number of church folks that would suddenly drop dead for esteeming money over the Messiah. Both in the pews and pulpits. You ought to thank God for His grace, mercy and patience.

CHAPTER 19

GOD'S FAVOUR (approval - kindness - grace)

"My son, forget not my law; but let thine heart keep my commandments: [2] For length of days, and long life, and peace, shall they add to thee. [3] Let not mercy and truth forsake thee: bind them about thy neck; write them upon the table of thine heart: [4] So shalt thou find favour and good understanding in the sight of God and man." *(Prov. 3:1-4)*

When you find God, you will find life and His favour (Prov. 8:35; John 10:10). As you continue to seek God, He will continue to pour out His favour on you (Prov. 11:27).

Queen Ester found favour with God

"And the king said unto Esther at the banquet of wine, What is thy petition? and it shall be granted thee: and what is thy request? even to the half of the kingdom it shall be performed. [7] Then answered Esther, and said, My petition and my request is; [8] If I have found favour in the sight of the king, and if it please the king to grant my petition, and to perform my request, let the king and Haman come to the banquet that I shall prepare for them, and I will do to morrow as the king hath said." *(Esth. 5:6-8)*

"For whoso findeth me findeth life, and shall obtain favour of the Lord." *(Prov. 8:35)*

For the righteous

Job:

"Thou hast granted me life and favour, and thy visitation hath preserved my spirit." *(Job 10:12)*

Mary:

"And the angel came in unto her, and said, Hail, thou that art highly favoured, the Lord is with thee: blessed art thou among women. [30] And the angel said unto her, Fear not, Mary: for thou hast found favour with God." *(Luke 1:28,30)*

David:

"Which also our fathers that came after brought in with Jesus into the possession of the Gentiles, whom God drave out before the face of our fathers, unto the days of David; [46] Who found favour before God, and desired to find a tabernacle for the God of Jacob." *(Acts 7:45-46)*

"A good man obtaineth favour of the Lord: but a man of wicked devices will he condemn." *(Prov. 12:2)*

"For thou, Lord, wilt bless the righteous; with favour wilt thou compass him as with a shield." *(Ps. 5:12)*

You can pray for God's favour to come to you

"Remember me, O Lord, with the favour that thou bearest unto thy people: O visit me with thy salvation." *(Ps. 106:4)*

"I intreated thy favour with my whole heart: be merciful unto me according to thy word." *(Ps. 119:58)*

Not for the wicked

"When the boughs thereof are withered, they shall be broken off: the women come, and set them on fire: for it is a people of no understanding: therefore he that made them will not have mercy on them, and he that formed them will shew them no favour." *(Is. 27:11)*

"Therefore will I cast you out of this land into a land that ye know not, neither ye nor your fathers; and there shall ye serve other gods day and night; where I will not shew you favour." *(Jer. 16:13)*

"Do ye think that the scripture saith in vain, The spirit that dwelleth in us lusteth to envy? [6] But he giveth more grace. Wherefore he saith, God resisteth the proud, but giveth grace unto the humble. [7] Submit yourselves therefore to God. Resist the devil, and he will flee from you. [8] Draw nigh to God, and he will draw nigh to you. Cleanse your hands, ye sinners; and purify your hearts, ye double minded. [9] Be afflicted, and mourn, and weep: let your laughter be turned to mourning, and your joy to heaviness. [10] Humble yourselves in the sight of the Lord, and he shall lift you up. [11] Speak not evil one of another, brethren. He that speaketh evil of his brother, and judgeth his brother, speaketh evil of the law, and judgeth the law: but if thou judge the law, thou art not a doer of the law, but a judge."
(James 4:5-11)

Others who found favour with God
(Samuel 1 Sam. 2:26)
(Joseph Gen. 39:2)
(Daniel Dan. 1:8-9, 6:3)
(Jesus Luke 2:52)

You can have the favour of God and man,
if you walk in God's mercy and truth

"Let not mercy and truth forsake thee: bind them about thy neck; write them upon the table of thine heart: [4] So shalt thou find favour and good understanding in the sight of God and man." *(Prov. 3:3-4)*

CHAPTER 20

A TRUE FRIEND

"A man that hath friends must shew himself friendly: and there is a friend that sticketh closer than a brother." *(Prov. 18:24)*

His name is Jesus.

You will find that one of the closest human friendship in the bible is the friendship of David & Jonathan. You can see this friendship in the book of 1 Samuel chapter 20.

Jesus explains the closeness of a friend to His disciples

"Greater love hath no man than this, that a man lay down his life for his friends. [14] Ye are my friends, if ye do whatsoever I command you. [15] Henceforth I call you not servants; for the servant knoweth not what his lord doeth: but I have called you friends; for all things that I have heard of my Father I have made known unto you." *(John 15:13-15)*

In the giving of the Great Commission to His disciples, Jesus explains to them the commitment of a true friend.

"Go ye therefore, and teach all nations, baptizing them in the name of the Father, and of the Son, and of the Holy Ghost: [20] Teaching them to observe all things whatsoever I have commanded you: and, lo, I am with you alway, even unto the end of the world. Amen." *(Matt. 28:19-20)*

Solomon said this of a true friend

"A friend loveth at all times, and a brother is born for adversity."
(Prov. 17:17)

"Faithful are the wounds of a friend; but the kisses of an enemy are deceitful." *(Prov. 27:6)*

"Iron sharpeneth iron; so a man sharpeneth the countenance of his friend." *(Prov. 27:17)*

You and your friend will help to mold and develop each other's character.

If you want to find out the quality of a relationship, let money be the distracting factor.

Jesus said this of the quality of a friend

"Greater love hath no man than this, that a man lay down his life for his friends." *(John 15:13)*

Would you lay down your life for a friend ?

A friend is one who loves at all times, regardless of what the situation or circumstance might be, they will be there for you unconditionally.
See Prov. 17:17

Examples of a few biblical genuine friendships

David and Jonathan. 1 Sam. 20:42

Ruth and Naomi. Ruth chapter one

Jesus and His Disciples. John 17:12

As a child of God, this is God's promise to you

"Who gave himself for our sins, that he might deliver us from this present evil world, according to the will of God and our Father." *(Gal. 1:4)*

"Being confident of this very thing, that he which hath begun a good work in you will perform it until the day of Jesus Christ." *(Phil. 1:6)*

This should be your attitude at all times

"And the Lord shall deliver me from every evil work, and will preserve me unto his heavenly kingdom: to whom be glory for ever and ever. Amen." *(2 Tim. 4:18)*

"What shall we then say to these things? If God be for us, who can be against us? [32] He that spared not his own Son, but delivered him up for us all, how shall he not with him also freely give us all things? [33] Who shall lay any thing to the charge of God's elect? It is God that justifieth. [34] Who is he that condemneth? It is Christ that died, yea rather, that is risen again, who is even at the right hand of God, who also maketh intercession for us. [35] Who shall separate us from the love of Christ? shall tribulation, or distress, or persecution, or famine, or nakedness, or peril, or sword? [36] As it is written, For thy sake we are killed all the day long; we are accounted as sheep for the slaughter. [37] Nay, in all these things we are more than conquerors through him that loved us. [38] For I am persuaded, that neither death, nor life, nor angels, nor principalities, nor powers, nor things present, nor things to come, [39] Nor height, nor depth, nor any other creature, shall be able to separate us from the love of God, which is in Christ Jesus our Lord." *(Rom. 8:31-39)*

CHAPTER 21

INTEGRITY

You have integrity when you have proven to possess an innocence or upright character before God.

Listen to what the wisest man that ever lived outside of Jesus said about integrity.

"A good name is better than precious ointment; and the day of death than the day of one's birth." *(Eccl. 7:1)*

"The just man walketh in his integrity: his children are blessed after him." *(Prov. 20:7)*

The price of integrity is a justified status before God.

"The integrity of the upright shall guide them: but the perverseness of transgressors shall destroy them." *(Prov. 11:3)*

"Better is the poor that walketh in his integrity, than he that is perverse in his lips, and is a fool." *(Prov. 19:1)*

"A good name is rather to be chosen than great riches, and loving favour rather than silver and gold." *(Prov. 22:1)*

Integrity is one of the factors David asked God to Judge him on.

"The Lord shall judge the people: judge me, O Lord, according to my righteousness, and according to mine integrity that is in me." *(Ps. 7:8)*

INTEGRITY

David says, this is how he was preserved

"Let integrity and uprightness preserve me; for I wait on thee." *(Ps. 25:21)*

It was said by Solomon: Money answers all things

"A feast is made for laughter, and wine maketh merry: but money aswereth all things." *(Eccl. 10:19)* *"Solomon's worldly viewpoint."*

However, Solomon went on to say:

"For wisdom is a defence, and money is a defence: but the excellency of knowledge is, that wisdom giveth life to them that have it. [13] Consider the work of God: for who can make that straight, which he hath made crooked? [14] In the day of prosperity be joyful, but in the day of adversity consider: God also hath set the one over against the other, to the end that man should find nothing after him." *(Eccl. 7:12-14)* Better said.

As the facts have shown in this book, based upon the word of God, money is not the answer to all things. However, if you use money wisely, it will help you to establish God's expected end for your life. See Jer. 29:11 NIV

Examples of men with great integrity.

Moses

"By faith Moses, when he was come to years, refused to be called the son of Pharaoh's daughter; [25] Choosing rather to suffer affliction with the people of God, than to enjoy the pleasures of sin for a season; [26] Esteeming the reproach of Christ greater riches than the treasures in Egypt: for he had respect unto the recompence of the reward. [27] By faith he forsook Egypt, not fearing the wrath of the king: for he endured, as seeing him who is invisible." *(Heb. 11:24-27)*

The reproach of Christ.

As a child of God, you must learn to stand for righteousness. Though the walk gets very tiring at times, it is still no excuse for you to comprise the word of God. You must do as the apostle Paul did. He kept his eyes on Jesus, despite the many opportunities to say yes to the enemy. He finished the race by keeping the faith.

"Let us go forth therefore unto him without the camp, bearing his reproach." *(Heb. 13:13)*

"Yea, and all that will live godly in Christ Jesus shall suffer persecution." *(2 Tim. 3:2)*

"If the Lord delight in us, then he will bring us into this land, and give it us; a land which floweth with milk and honey." *(Num. 14:8)*

Joseph

"And Joseph was brought down to Egypt; and Potiphar, an officer of Pharaoh, captain of the guard, an Egyptian, bought him of the hands of the Ishmeelites, which had brought him down thither. [2] And the Lord was with Joseph, and he was a prosperous man; and he was in the house of his master the Egyptian. [3] And his master saw that the Lord was with him, and that the Lord made all that he did to prosper in his hand. [4] And Joseph found grace in his sight, and he served him: and he made him overseer over his house, and all that he had he put into his hand." *(Gen. 39:1-4)*

"But the Lord was with Joseph, and shewed him mercy, and gave him favour in the sight of the keeper of the prison. [22] And the keeper of the prison committed to Joseph's hand all the prisoners that were in the prison; and whatsoever they did there, he was the doer of it. [23] The keeper of the prison looked not to any thing that was under his hand; because the Lord was with him, and that which he did, the Lord made it to prosper." *(Gen. 39:21-23)*

Job

"And the Lord said unto Satan, Hast thou considered my servant Job, that there is none like him in the earth, a perfect and an upright man, one that feareth God, and escheweth evil? and still he holdeth fast his integrity, although thou movedst me against him, to destroy him without cause." *(Job 2:3)*

"Then said his wife unto him, Dost thou still retain thine integrity? curse God, and die. [10] But he said unto her, Thou speakest as one of the foolish women speaketh. What? shall we receive good at the hand of God, and shall we not receive evil? In all this did not Job sin with his lips." *(Job 2:9-10)*

"And said, Naked came I out of my mother's womb, and naked shall I return thither: the Lord gave, and the Lord hath taken away; blessed be the name of the Lord." *(Job 1:21)*

Paul

"I am crucified with Christ: nevertheless I live; yet not I, but Christ liveth in me: and the life which I now live in the flesh I live by the faith of the Son of God, who loved me, and gave himself for me." *(Gal. 2:20)*

Jesus

"For we have not an high priest which cannot be touched with the feeling of our infirmities; but was in all points tempted like as we are, yet without sin." *(Heb. 4:15)*

"For even hereunto were ye called: because Christ also suffered for us, leaving us an example, that ye should follow his steps." *(1 Pet. 2:21)*

"Yea, and all that will live godly in Christ Jesus shall suffer persecution." *(2 Tim. 3:12)*

Moses and Aaron's plea to the children of Israel to not rebel against God. This assured them of not having to compromise their character with the enemy.

"If the Lord delight in us, then he will bring us into this land, and give it us; a land which floweth with milk and honey. [9] Only rebel not ye against the Lord, neither fear ye the people of the land; for they are bread for us: their defence is departed from them, and the Lord is with us: fear them not." *(Num. 14:8-9)*

CHAPTER 22

QUENCHABLE THIRST

All the things money can buy without Jesus - will not fill that empty void. God made you in His image and likeness and only He can make you whole. You must come to realize that the things God created on this earth are not evil. You sin when things are used in an unrighteous manner. When this happens, the enemy tricks you into letting things such as money become your god. God does not want you to do anything to His temple that will defile it. Money in itself will never quench your thirst (Eccl. 4:8,5:10). The whole world is emptiness without God - therefore, you can only live a complete and satisified life in the deity of God through Christ (Eph. 2:12; Col. 2:6-15). God made you for eternity - therefore, temporal things such as money will not satisfy an eternal thirst (Eccl. 3:11 NIV).

Only God can satisfy your inner thirst

"For he satisfieth the longing soul, and filleth the hungry soul with goodness." *(Ps.107:9)* See also. Ps. 42:2,63:1,65:4,84:2,105:40,119:20,143:6; Jer. 31:14; Ezek. 7:14-19; Matt. 22:37; James. 5:5; Ps. 36:8-9

Jesus spoke the following words about Satan (devil).

"The thief cometh not, but for to steal, and to kill, and to destroy: I am come that they might have life, and that they might have it more abundantly." *(John 10:10)*

If you are involved in afflicting yourself with anything that devalues your life, it is not of God. It is from the devil, and you need deliverance from that unclean spirit. The devil is an illusionist. He wants you to think that he has the answer for quenching your thirst. Remember, he did not make you. God created you in His image and likeness. God is the only one who can quench that thirst. Hallelujah!

"Circumcise yourselves to the Lord, and take away the foreskins of your heart, ye men of Judah and inhabitants of Jerusalem: lest my fury come forth like fire, and burn that none can quench it, because of the evil of your doings." *(Jer. 4:4)*

"For in him dwelleth all the fulness of the Godhead bodily. [10] And ye are complete in him, which is the head of all principality and power."
(Col. 2:9-10)

Satan is an illusionist. He offers you the following type of things to try and satisfy you.

The following is a partial list of things that most people try to quench that thirst they have. However, they find that nothing seems to satisfy that emptiness.

Alcohol. Be not drunk with a heathen spirit, but with the Holy Spirit.

If you are a Christian reading this book, meditate on these verses concerning abstaining from this weight and or sin. Drunkenness is a work of the flesh.

"Wine is a mocker, strong drink is raging: and whosoever is deceived thereby is not wise." (Prov. 20:1) See also. Prov. 31:7

"For the drunkard and the glutton shall come to poverty: and drowsiness shall clothe a man with rags." (Prov. 23:21)

"Who hath woe? who hath sorrow? who hath contentions? who hath babbling? who hath wounds without cause? who hath redness of eyes? [30] They that tarry long at the wine; they that go to seek mixed wine."
(Prov. 23:29-30)

"Envyings, murders, drunkenness, revellings, and such like: of the which I tell you before, as I have also told you in time past, that they which do such things shall not inherit the kingdom of God." (Gal. 5:21)

"Wherefore seeing we also are compassed about with so great a cloud of witnesses, let us lay aside every weight, and the sin which doth so easily beset us, and let us run with patience the race that is set before us."
(Heb. 12:1)

"Abstain from all appearance of evil." (1 Thess. 5:22)

"And be not drunk with wine, wherein is excess; but be filled with the Spirit." *(Eph. 5:18)*

"It is good neither to eat flesh, nor to drink wine, nor any thing whereby thy brother stumbleth, or is offended, or is made weak." *(Rom. 14:21)*

"What? know ye not that your body is the temple of the Holy Ghost which is in you, which ye have of God, and ye are not your own. [20] For ye are bought with a price: therefore glorify God in your body, and in your spirit, which are God's." *(1 Cor. 6:19-20)*   See also. Luke 21:34; Rom. 13:13; Is. 28:7; Ezek. 23:32, 39:19

Men.

"Young men likewise exhort to be sober minded. [7] In all things shewing thyself a pattern of good works: in doctrine shewing uncorruptness, gravity, sincerity, [8] Sound speech, that cannot be condemned; that he that is of the contrary part may be ashamed, having no evil thing to say of you." *(Titus 2:6-8)*   Religious leaders: Lev. 10:9 NIV; Is. 28:7 NIV; Eph. 5:18 NIV

See also. Lev. 10:8-11; Num. 6:1-3; Titus 1:7-8,2:2; Luke 1:15;
1 Tim. 3:1-3

Women.

"That they may teach the young women to be sober, to love their husbands, to love their children, [5] To be discreet, chaste, keepers at home, good, obedient to their own husbands, that the word of God be not blasphemed." *(Titus 2:4-5)* See also. 1 Tim. 2:9,3:11

"Therefore let us not sleep, as do others; but let us watch and be sober." *(1 Thess. 5:6)* See additional reference. 1 Thess. 5:7-8

"Teaching us that, denying ungodliness and worldly lusts, we should live soberly, righteously, and godly, in this present world." *(Titus 2:12)*

"But the end of all things is at hand: be ye therefore sober, and watch unto prayer." *(1 Pet. 4:7)*

"Be sober, be vigilant; because your adversary the devil, as a roaring lion, walketh about, seeking whom he may devour." *(1 Pet. 5:8)*

Drunkenness can lead to things such as:

1. Sexual sins.

   "Look not thou upon the wine when it is red, when it giveth his colour in the cup, when it moveth itself aright. [32] At the last it biteth like a serpent, and stingeth like an adder. [33] Thine eyes shall behold strange women, and thine heart shall utter perverse things."*(Prov. 23:31-33)*   See also. Gen. 19:30-38

2. Ungodly words. Prov. 6:2,18:21,23:33; Matt. 12:37; James 3:2,6

3. Strongholds (bondages of many different unclean spirits).
   "They have stricken me, shalt thou say, and I was not sick; they have beaten me, and I felt it not: when shall I awake? I will seek it yet again." *(Prov. 23:35)*

Death.

   There are more than 100,000 alcohol related deaths in the United States each year. They are deaths in the area of automobile; firearms; newborns; homicides; suicides; cancer; strokes; and alcohol related diseases. Source - NHTSA.

"Yea also, because he transgresseth by wine, he is a proud man, neither keepeth at home, who enlargeth his desire as hell, and is as death, and cannot be satisfied, but gathereth unto him all nations, and heapeth unto him all people." *(Hab. 2:5)*

See also. Prov. 21:17,23:20-21,29-35;Is. 28:1,65:8;Hos. 4:11; Matt. 24:49; Rom. 13:13; 1 Cor. 5:11,6:10,10:31,11:21; 1 Thess. 5:7-8; Gal. 5:19-21,24

"A little leaven leaveneth the whole lump." *(Gal. 5:9)*

THINGS MONEY CAN'T BUY

Drugs.

They are unclean spirits. They allow you to illegally enter into the spirit realm. When you enter in this way, you will enter into the unholy spirit realm. You open yourself up to the area of spiritual darkness. This is the enemy's battleground. This is a violation of the word of God (Rev. 9:21, 18:23, 21:8, 22:15).

These are spirits of escape that must be (cast out) not (counsel out), for deliverance.

Sex.

Solomon found that sex could not fill this void.
"Neither shall he multiply wives to himself, that his heart turn not away: neither shall he greatly multiply to himself silver and gold. *(Deut. 17:17)*

"And he had seven hundred wives, princesses, and three hundred concubines: and his wives turned away his heart. [4] For it came to pass, when Solomon was old, that his wives turned away his heart after other gods: and his heart was not perfect with the Lord his God, as was the heart of David his father." *(1 Kgs. 11:3-4)*

Sex is a pleasure that God ordained. However, God only means for it to take place between a 'married male man and his female wife'.

"Therefore shall a man leave his father and his mother, and shall cleave unto his wife: and they shall be one flesh." *(Gen. 2:24)*

"Nevertheless, to avoid fornication, let every man have his own wife, and let every woman have her own husband." *(1 Cor. 7:2)*

"And God said, Let us make man in our image, after our likeness: and let them have dominion over the fish of the sea, and over the fowl of the air, and over the cattle, and over all the earth, and over every creeping thing that creepeth upon the earth. [27] So God created man in his own image, in the image of God created he him; male and female created he them. [28] And God blessed them, and God said unto them, Be fruitful, and multiply, and replenish the earth, and subdue it: and have dominion over the fish of the sea, and over the fowl of the air, and over every living thing that moveth upon the earth." *(Gen. 1:26-28)*

"Thou shalt not lie with mankind, as with womankind: it is abomination. [23] Neither shalt thou lie with any beast to defile thyself therewith: neither shall any woman stand before a beast to lie down thereto: it is confusion. [24] Defile not ye yourselves in any of these things: for in all these the nations are defiled which I cast out before you: [25] And the land is defiled: therefore I do visit the iniquity thereof upon it, and the land itself vomiteth out her inhabitants. [26] Ye shall therefore keep my statutes and my judgments, and shall not commit any of these abominations; neither any of your own nation, nor any stranger that sojourneth among you." *(Lev. 18:22-26)*

"If a man also lie with mankind, as he lieth with a woman, both of them have committed an abomination: they shall surely be put to death; their blood shall be upon them." *(Lev. 20:13)*

"Know ye not that the unrighteous shall not inherit the kingdom of God? Be not deceived: neither fornicators, nor idolaters, nor adulterers, nor effeminate, nor abusers of themselves with mankind, [10] Nor thieves, nor covetous, nor drunkards, nor revilers, nor extortioners, shall inherit the kingdom of God. [11] And such were some of you: but ye are washed, but ye are sanctified, but ye are justified in the name of the Lord Jesus, and by the Spirit of our God." *(1 Cor. 6:9-11)*

The story of Sodom and Gomorrah.

"And the Lord said, Because the cry of Sodom and Gomorrah is great, and because their sin is very grievous." *(Gen. 18:20)*

"Then the Lord rained upon Sodom and upon Gomorrah brimstone and fire from the Lord out of heaven." *(Gen. 19:24)*

Read the book of Romans chapter one, for further understanding.

"For as a young man marrieth a virgin, so shall thy sons marry thee: and as the bridegroom rejoiceth over the bride, so shall thy God rejoice over thee." *(Is. 62:5)*

"And said, For this cause shall a man leave father and mother, and shall cleave to his wife: and they twain shall be one flesh." *(Matt. 19:5)*

"For this cause shall a man leave his father and mother, and cleave to his wife." *(Mark 10:7)*

"Wherefore they are no more twain, but one flesh. What therefore God hath joined together, let not man put asunder." *(Matt. 19:6)*

Worldly honour.

"What is man, that thou art mindful of him? and the son of man, that thou visitest him? For thou hast made him a little lower than the angels, and hast crowned him with glory and honour." *(Ps. 8:4-5)*

"Man that is in honour, and understandeth not, is like the beasts that perish." *(Ps. 49:20)*

"He that followeth after righteousness and mercy findeth life, righteousness, and honour." *(Prov. 21:21)*

When you are walking in worldly honour, God is not pleased. However, He will let you know when He is pleased with you.

"For he received from God the Father honour and glory, when there came such a voice to him from the excellent glory, This is my beloved Son, in whom I am well pleased." *(2 Pet. 1:7)*

Vain honor and glory.

This leads to a spirit of arrogance.

"For that ye ought to say, If the Lord will, we shall live, and do this, or that. [16] But now ye rejoice in your boastings: all such rejoicing is evil. [17] Therefore to him that knoweth to do good, and doeth it not, to him it is sin." *(James 4:15-17)*

"Let us not be desirous of vain glory, provoking one another, envying one another." *(Gal. 5:26)*   See also. Is. 5:8-10; Jer. 9:23-24

Read 1 Chronicles 29:12 and Proverbs 3:16 for the source of true honor.

"Thou madest him a little lower than the angels; thou crownedst him with glory and honour, and didst set him over the works of thy hands: [8] Thou hast put all things in subjection under his feet. For in that he put all in subjection under him, he left nothing that is not put under him. But now we see not yet all things put under him." *(Heb. 2:7-8)*

See also. John 7:18

Education.

Paul of Tarsus.

"I am verily a man which am a Jew, born in Tarsus, a city in Cilicia, yet brought up in this city at the feet of Gamaliel, and taught according to the perfect manner of the law of the fathers, and was zealous toward God, as ye all are this day. And I persecuted this way unto the death, binding and delivering into prisons both men and women." *(Acts 22:3-4)*

Paul no doubt was a very educated man. His education could not satisfy that inner thirst. Therefore, the enemy used this worldly wisdom to kill, steal and destroy the children of God. However, he had not experienced a life changing encounter with Jesus. Paul was one of many who had been spiritually blinded by God, because of his disobedience.

In the book of Isaiah and 1 Corinthian, God promised He would destroy worldly wisdom.

"Therefore, behold, I will proceed to do a marvellous work among this people, even a marvellous work and a wonder: for the wisdom of their wise men shall perish, and the understanding of their prudent men shall be hid." *(Is. 29:14)*

"For it is written, I will destroy the wisdom of the wise, and will bring to nothing the understanding of the prudent." *(1 Cor. 1:19)*

THINGS MONEY CAN'T BUY

This promise was fulfilled by God.

"Where is the wise? where is the scribe? where is the disputer of this world? hath not God made foolish the wisdom of this world."
(1 Cor. 1:20)

For those of you who think that the wisdom of this world will satisfy your inner thirst, meditate of these words of God.

"That, according as it is written, He that glorieth, let him glory in the Lord."
(1 Cor. 1:31)

"For what man knoweth the things of a man, save the spirit of man which is in him? even so the things of God knoweth no man, but the Spirit of God."
(1 Cor. 2:11)

"For the wisdom of this world is foolishness with God. For it is written, He taketh the wise in their own craftiness." *(1 Cor. 3:19)*

"But the natural man receiveth not the things of the Spirit of God: for they are foolishness unto him: neither can he know them, because they are spiritually discerned." *(1 Cor. 2:14)* See also. Eph. 4:18

The answer is - You must be born again. Read the story of Nicodemus in the third chapter of John verses one through twenty one.

If you do not yield to the word of God, God will do to you what He did to the children of Israel.

"For the Lord hath poured out upon you the spirit of deep sleep, and hath closed your eyes: the prophets and your rulers, the seers hath he covered." *(Is. 29:10)* See additional reference. Matt. 13:15

You will fall into the trap of the enemy as did Solomon and Paul.

"There is a way which seemeth right unto a man, but the end thereof are the ways of death." *(Prov. 14:12)*

"Though I might also have confidence in the flesh. If any other man thinketh that he hath whereof he might trust in the flesh, I more: [5] Circumcised the eighth day, of the stock of Israel, of the tribe of Benjamin, an Hebrew of the Hebrews; as touching the law, a Pharisee; [6] Concerning zeal, persecuting the church; touching the righteousness which is in the law, blameless. [7] But what things were gain to me, those I counted loss for Christ."
(Phil. 3:4-7)

"Who was before a blasphemer, and a persecutor, and injurious: but I obtained mercy, because I did it ignorantly in unbelief." *(1 Tim. 1:13)*

"And as he journeyed, he came near Damascus: and suddenly there shined round about him a light from heaven: [4] And he fell to the earth, and heard a voice saying unto him, Saul, Saul, why persecutest thou me?"
(Acts 9:3-4)

"And he said, Who art thou, Lord? And the Lord said, I am Jesus whom thou persecutest: it is hard for thee to kick against the pricks." *(Acts 9:5)*

"And Ananias went his way, and entered into the house; and putting his hands on him said, Brother Saul, the Lord, even Jesus, that appeared unto thee in the way as thou camest, hath sent me, that thou mightest receive thy sight, and be filled with the Holy Ghost." *(Acts 9:17)*

"And immediately there fell from his eyes as it had been scales: and he received sight forthwith, and arose, and was baptized." *(Acts 9:18)*

"(According as it is written, God hath given them the spirit of slumber, eyes that they should not see, and ears that they should not hear;) unto this day."
(Rom. 11:8)

"For this people's heart is waxed gross, and their ears are dull of hearing, and their eyes they have closed; lest at any time they should see with their eyes, and hear with their ears, and should understand with their heart, and should be converted, and I should heal them." *(Matt. 13:15)*

After his encounter with Jesus.

"Yea doubtless, and I count all things but loss for the excellency of the knowledge of Christ Jesus my Lord: for whom I have suffered the loss of all things, and do count them but dung, that I may win Christ." *(Phil. 3:8)*

False gods (idol worship).

God is a jealous God

"Thou shalt not bow down thyself to them, nor serve them: for I the Lord thy God am a jealous God, visiting the iniquity of the fathers upon the children unto the third and fourth generation of them that hate me." *(Ex. 20:5)*

Be aware of generational curses. Ever wonder why certain sinful habits seem to run in the family. These spirits can be destroyed (Lam. 5:7; 2:14; Jer. 31:29-30; Ezek. 18:1-4,20).

"For the Lord thy God is a consuming fire, even a jealous God."
(Deut. 4:24)

When you make God number one in your life, His consuming power will destroy every false god in your life.

The kingdom of God rules over the kingdom of this world.
See additional reference. Ezekiel chapter seventeen.

"(For the Lord thy God is a jealous God among you) lest the anger of the Lord thy God be kindled against thee, and destroy thee from off the face of The earth." *(Deut. 6:15)*

Sports.

"But refuse profane and old wives' fables, and exercise thyself rather unto godliness. [8] For bodily exercise profiteth little: but godliness is profitable unto all things, having promise of the life that now is, and of that which is to come." *(1 Tim. 4:7-8)*

"Know ye not that they which run in a race run all, but one receiveth the prize? So run, that ye may obtain." *(1 Cor. 9:24)*

"And ye are complete in him, which is the head of all principality and power." *(Col. 2:10)*

This is a typical comment concerning not just sports but many things in this world. "I love ???? more than life itself". This should not be so. This is an idol god.

You are commanded not to place anything or anyone before God.

"Who changed the truth of God into a lie, and worshipped and served the creature more than the Creator, who is blessed for ever. Amen."
(Rom. 1:25)

"He feedeth on ashes: a deceived heart hath turned him aside, that he cannot deliver his soul, nor say, Is there not a lie in my right hand?"
(Is. 44:20)

"Every man is brutish in his knowledge: every founder is confounded by the graven image: for his molten image is falsehood, and there is no breath in them." *(Jer. 10:14)*

"Thou shalt have no other gods before me." *(Ex. 20:3)*

"Jesus said unto him, Thou shalt love the Lord thy God with all thy heart, and with all thy soul, and with all thy mind." *(Matt. 22:37)*

Fame. Many famous people have died spiritually disconnected from God.

"For what is a man profited, if he shall gain the whole world, and lose his own soul? or what shall a man give in exchange for his soul ?"
(Matt. 16:26)

"The blessing of the Lord, it maketh rich, and he addeth no sorrow with it."
(Prov. 10:22)

THINGS MONEY CAN'T BUY

Material things.

"Then I looked on all the works that my hands had wrought, and on the labour that I had laboured to do: and, behold, all was vanity and vexation of spirit, and there was no profit under the sun." *(Eccl. 2:11)*

Religion. The only religion that is true, is your obedient relationship with the living God. All other religions are vain (empty-an idol).

"Pure religion and undefiled before God and the Father is this, To visit the fatherless and widows in their affliction, and to keep himself unspotted from the world." *(James 1:27)*

Vain religion can be bought.

"Be not carried about with divers and strange doctrines. For it is a good thing that the heart be established with grace; not with meats, which have not profited them that have been occupied therein." *(Heb. 13:9)*

Worldly power. The kingdoms of this world are not able to quench any thirst you are faced with. These kingdoms consist of things that you esteem more than God. The secular educational system(intellectualism); religious; economical; and cultural systems etc.

"By thy great wisdom and by thy traffick hast thou increased thy riches, and thine heart is lifted up because of thy riches." *(Ezek. 28:5)*

"This I say then, Walk in the Spirit, and ye shall not fulfil the lust of the flesh. [17] For the flesh lusteth against the Spirit, and the Spirit against the flesh: and these are contrary the one to the other: so that ye cannot do the things that ye would." *(Gal. 5:16-17)*

"For all that is in the world, the lust of the flesh, and the lust of the eyes, and the pride of life, is not of the Father, but is of the world. [17] And the world passeth away, and the lust thereof: but he that doeth the will of God abideth for ever." *(1 John 2:16-17)*

"He that hath no rule over his own spirit is like a city that is broken down, and without walls." *(Prov. 25:28)*

Gambling. This is a spirit of covetousness – a desire of pursuing worldly things. Even when you are winning, you will never be satisfied.

"He that loveth silver shall not be satisfied with silver; nor he that loveth abundance with increase: this is also vanity." *(Eccl. 5:10)*

"For this ye know, that no whoremonger, nor unclean person, nor covetous man, who is an idolater, hath any inheritance in the kingdom of Christ and of God." *(Eph. 5:5)*

"Mortify therefore your members which are upon the earth; fornication, uncleanness, inordinate affection, evil concupiscence, and covetousness, which is idolatry." *(Col. 3:5)*   If not, this is the end result. Rev. 21:8

"Thou shalt have no other gods before me." *(Ex. 20:3)* See. Deut. 7:25-26

"But they that will be rich fall into temptation and a snare, and into many foolish and hurtful lusts, which drown men in destruction and perdition." *(1 Tim. 6:9)*   Read 1 Tim. 6:10.

"Wealth gotten by vanity shall be diminished: but he that gathereth by labour shall increase." *(Prov. 13:11)* See also. Amplified version

"Treasures of wickedness profit nothing: but righteousness delivereth from death." *(Prov. 10:2)*

"Let your conversation be without covetousness; and be content with such things as ye have: for he hath said, I will never leave thee, nor forsake thee." *(Heb. 13:5)*

In the book of Psalms 10:3 of the Amplified Version, you will find that the person with this spirit curses, despises and renounces the Lord Himself.

Gambling should be hated and rejected by all saints, as like Paul.

"I have coveted no man's silver, or gold, or apparel." *(Acts 20:33)*

God hates income received from the spirit of covetousness (Psalms 10:3).

Ungodly music. Take heed to what you hear (Mark 4:24; Luke 8:16-18).

If whatever you are singing or listening to is not glorifying God, it is glorifying the devil. This is a vexation of your spirit. If the music is anointed, people are spiritually blessed. If it is not, people are tormented. See the story of Saul and David (1 Sam. 16:14-17,23) and Solomon (Eccl. 2:8,10,11).

Listening to this type of music will cause you to worship idol gods. Read the third chapter of Daniel for clarification.

"Speaking to yourselves in psalms and hymns and spiritual songs, singing and making melody in your heart to the Lord." *(Eph. 5:19)*

See. Ps. 95:2, 119:54-56 (Holy Songs from the Word of God)

"Let the word of Christ dwell in you richly in all wisdom; teaching and admonishing one another in psalms and hymns and spiritual songs, singing with grace in your hearts to the Lord." *(Col. 3:16)*

Even singing in the Spirit.

"What is it then? I will pray with the spirit, and I will pray with the understanding also: I will sing with the spirit, and I will sing with the understanding also. [16] Else when thou shalt bless with the spirit, how shall he that occupieth the room of the unlearned say Amen at thy giving of thanks, seeing he understandeth not what thou sayest." *(1 Cor. 14:15-16)*

"Ye adulterers and adulteresses, know ye not that the friendship of the world is enmity with God? whosoever therefore will be a friend of the world is the enemy of God." *(James 4:4)*

"If ye were of the world, the world would love his own: but because ye are not of the world, but I have chosen you out of the world, therefore the world hateth you." *(John 15:19)*

"Love not the world, neither the things that are in the world. If any man love the world, the love of the Father is not in him. [16] For all that is in the world, the lust of the flesh, and the lust of the eyes, and the pride of life, is not of the Father, but is of the world. [17] And the world passeth away, and the lust thereof: but he that doeth the will of God abideth for ever." *(1 John 2:15-17)*

See additional references.
Ex. 15:1-2; Job 31:1; Ps. 24:4; Is. 26:1, 42:10; Matt. 5:28,16:26,26:30; Luke 21:34-36; John 12:25; Rom. 12:2; 1 Cor 3:16-17; Gal. 6:14; Col. 2:20; 2 Pet. 1:4; 2 Pet. 2:20; Rev. 15:3; Amos 5:23,6:1-11; Is. 5:12,14:11; Ezek. 26:13

How to quench your thirst

Let us look at the story of the deliverance of the children of Israel. God delivered them out of Egypt. Egypt is a type of the world. You must first be born again. You have to receive Jesus Christ as your personal Saviour. Secondly, God began to deliver the children of Israel through the wilderness. He feed them physically with meat, bread and water. The spiritual aspect of this deliverance was their deliverance from their dry places (bondages) – things being used to substitute for God. Thirdly, God brought them to Canaan (promise land).

Even in the promise land, God had to drive out all the enemies (ammonites, jebusites, hittites, all the -ites-) for them to live a victorious life. Once you are born again, you must receive transformation of your soul. This is where the dry places are. These dry places are nothing but weights and sins.

To satisfy your thirst, you must:

1. Leave Egypt. Receive the gift of salvation. Your soul must thirst for the living God. Ex. 15:1-2;Ps. 107:9; Is. 5:13;1 Cor. 12:13;Rev 7:16-17,18:4

2. Be transformed by continuing to thirst and drink the living word of God - spiritual sustenance. Ex. 17:6; Num. 20:11; Ps. 36:8,78:15; Prov. 13:14,14:27; Is. 55:1-3; Is. 58:11; John 6:35; 1 Cor. 10:4

THINGS MONEY CAN'T BUY

Drink from the Fountain-of-Continuous-Life-Giving-Water (Jesus) through the ministry of the Holy Ghost

"In the last day, that great day of the feast, Jesus stood and cried, saying, If any man thirst, let him come unto me, and drink. [38] He that believeth on me, as the scripture hath said, out of his belly shall flow rivers of living water. [39] (But this spake he of the Spirit, which they that believe on him should receive: for the Holy Ghost was not yet given; because that Jesus was not yet glorified." *(John 7:37-39)* See also. Ps. 36:9; Is. 30:21; Ezek. 36:27; John 4:1-15,10:10; Rom. 8:4-5,10,11; Eph 5:18; Rev. 7:17,22:1,17

David's continuous thirst for the living water
Ps. 42:1-2,63:1,84:2,143:6

Start living your new life hidden with Christ in God through the Holy Ghost

See references:
Matt. 5:6,6:33; Col. 3:1-3; 1 John 5:11-12; Gal. 5:16-26;
Acts 17:28-29; Heb. 1:3; 1 Pet. 2:24; Col. 2:9-10; 2 Cor. 5:17-18;
1 John 2:6; Rom. 1:16-17; 1 John 1:7; Gal. 2:20; Rom. 8:12-13;
Col. 3:5-10

"For my people have committed two evils; they have forsaken me the fountain of living waters, and hewed them out cisterns, broken cisterns, that can hold no water." (Jer. 2:13)

Without God in your life - you will never be able to quench that empty feeling

Ps. 16:11, 17:15

147

QUENCHABLE THIRST

Remember, earthly riches by themselves are not satisfying

"There is one alone, and there is not a second; yea, he hath neither child nor brother: yet is there no end of all his labour; neither is his eye satisfied with riches; neither saith he, For whom do I labour, and bereave my soul of good? This is also vanity, yea, it is a sore travail." *(Eccl. 4:8)*

CHAPTER 23

SATISFACTION (complete fulfillment)

David knew what or who could satisfy man

"How excellent is thy lovingkindness, O God! therefore the children of men put their trust under the shadow of thy wings. [8] They shall be abundantly satisfied with the fatness of thy house; and thou shalt make them drink of the river of thy pleasures." *(Ps. 36:7-8)*

The children of Satan will never be satisfied

"From men which are thy hand, O Lord, from men of the world, which have their portion in this life, and whose belly thou fillest with thy hid treasure: they are full of children, and leave the rest of their substance to their babes." *(Ps. 17:14)*

God's Provisions for the satisfaction of His children

"With long life will I satisfy him, and shew him my salvation." *(Ps. 91:16)*

"They shall not be ashamed in the evil time: and in the days of famine they shall be satisfied." *(Ps. 37:19)*

"Blessed is the man whom thou choosest, and causest to approach unto thee, that he may dwell in thy courts: we shall be satisfied with the good-ness of thy house, even of thy holy temple." *(Ps. 65:4)*

"And a man shall be as an hiding place from the wind, and a covert from the tempest; as rivers of water in a dry place, as the shadow of a great rock in a weary land." *(Is. 32:2)*

"For I will pour water upon him that is thirsty, and floods upon the dry ground: I will pour my spirit upon thy seed, and my blessing upon thine offspring." *(Is. 44:3)*

"Wherefore do ye spend money for that which is not bread? and your labour for that which satisfieth not? hearken diligently unto me, and eat ye that which is good, and let your soul delight itself in fatness." *(Is. 55:2)*

"And I will satiate the soul of the priests with fatness, and my people shall be satisfied with my goodness, saith the Lord." *(Jer. 31:14)*

For those who bear His image & likeness

"As for me, I will behold thy face in righteousness: I shall be satisfied, when I awake, with thy likeness." *(Ps. 17:15)*

The Samaritan woman @ the well meeting Jesus

"When therefore the Lord knew how the Pharisees had heard that Jesus made and baptized more disciples than John, [2] (Though Jesus himself baptized not, but his disciples,) [3] He left Judaea, and departed again into Galilee. [4] And he must needs go through Samaria. [5] Then cometh he to a city of Samaria, which is called Sychar, near to the parcel of ground that Jacob gave to his son Joseph. [6] Now Jacob's well was there. Jesus therefore, being wearied with his journey, sat thus on the well: and it was about the sixth hour. [7] There cometh a woman of Samaria to draw water: Jesus saith unto her, Give me to drink. [8] (For his disciples were gone away unto the city to buy meat.) [9] Then saith the woman of Samaria unto him, How is it that thou, being a Jew, askest drink of me, which am a woman of Samaria? for the Jews have no dealings with the Samaritans. [10] Jesus answered and said unto her, If thou knewest the gift of God, and who it is that saith to thee, Give me to drink; thou wouldest have asked of him, and he would have given thee living water. [11] The woman saith unto him, Sir, thou hast nothing to draw with, and the well is deep: from whence then hast thou that living water? [12] Art thou greater than our father Jacob, which gave us the well, and drank thereof himself, and his children, and his cattle? [13] Jesus answered and said unto her, Whosoever drinketh of this water shall thirst again." *(John 4:1-13)*

THINGS MONEY CAN'T BUY

Moses knew that he could not be satisfied with anything, without God

"By faith Moses, when he was come to years, refused to be called the son of Pharaoh's daughter; [25] Choosing rather to suffer affliction with the people of God, than to enjoy the pleasures of sin for a season; [26] Esteeming the reproach of Christ greater riches than the treasures in Egypt: for he had respect unto the recompence of the reward. [27] By faith he forsook Egypt, not fearing the wrath of the king: for he endured, as seeing him who is invisible." *(Heb. 11:24-27)*

Solomon knew that if God was not number one in his life, he could never be satisfied, even being the richest man in the world

"There is one alone, and there is not a second; yea, he hath neither child nor brother: yet is there no end of all his labour; neither is his eye satisfied with riches; neither saith he, For whom do I labour, and bereave my soul of good? This is also vanity, yea, it is a sore travail." *(Eccl. 4:8)*
See also. (Prov. 27:20,24)

"If thou seest the oppression of the poor, and violent perverting of judgment and justice in a province, marvel not at the matter: for he that is higher than the highest regardeth; and there be higher than they. [9] Moreover the profit of the earth is for all: the king himself is served by the field. [10] He that loveth silver shall not be satisfied with silver; nor he that loveth abundance with increase: this is also vanity. [11] When goods increase, they are increased that eat them: and what good is there to the owners thereof, saving the beholding of them with their eyes? [12] The sleep of a labouring man is sweet, whether he eat little or much: but the abundance of the rich will not suffer him to sleep. [13] There is a sore evil which I have seen under the sun, namely, riches kept for the owners thereof to their hurt. [14] But those riches perish by evil travail: and he begetteth a son, and there is nothing in his hand. [15] As he came forth of his mother's womb, naked shall he return to go as he came, and shall take nothing of his labour, which he may carry away in his hand. [16] And this also is a sore evil, that in all points as he came, so shall he go: and what profit hath he that hath laboured for the wind? [17] All his days also he eateth in darkness, and he hath much sorrow and wrath with his sickness. [18] Behold that which I have seen: it is good and comely for one to eat and to drink, and to enjoy the good of all his labour that he taketh under the sun all the days of his life,   which God giveth him: for it is his portion. [19] Every man also to whom God hath given riches and wealth, and hath given him power to eat thereof, and to take his portion, and to rejoice in his labour; this is the gift of God. [20] For he shall not much remember the days of his life; because God answereth him in the joy of his heart." *(Eccl. 5:8-20)*

Your soul (spiritual), is thirsting for the true God (Ps. 42:2). Therefore, nothing else can satisfy this thirst. Why not accept God's invitation to quench this thirst.

"Ho, every one that thirsteth, come ye to the waters, and he that hath no money; come ye, buy, and eat; yea, come, buy wine and milk without money and without price. [2] Wherefore do ye spend money for that which is not bread? and your labour for that which satisfieth not? hearken diligently unto me, and eat ye that which is good, and let your soul delight itself in fatness. [3] Incline your ear, and come unto me: hear, and your soul shall live; and I will make an everlasting covenant with you, even the sure mercies of David." *(Is. 55:1-3)*

CHAPTER 24

WISDOM OF GOD

The ability to practically apply what you know and understand !
Prov. 8:14,23 24:3-4 AMP

The wisest man that ever lived - outside of Jesus - had this to say about wisdom.

"Happy is the man that findeth wisdom, and the man that getteth understanding. [14] For the merchandise of it is better than the merchandise of silver, and the gain thereof than fine gold. [15] She is more precious than rubies: and all the things thou canst desire are not to be compared unto her." *(Prov. 3:13-15)*

It is evident in the word of God - that money can't buy the wisdom of God.

"If any of you lack wisdom, let him ask of God, that giveth to all men liberally, and upbraideth not; and it shall be <u>given</u> him." *(James 1:5)*

You do not have to bow to the wisdom of the world to be prosperous. This is devilish wisdom. God's wisdom is not of the world.

"The fear of the Lord is the beginning of wisdom: a good understanding have all they that do his commandments: his praise endureth for ever."
(Ps. 111:10)

"The fear of the Lord is the beginning of wisdom: and the knowledge of the holy is understanding." *(Prov. 9:10)*

Listen to what David said about trusting God

"I have been young, and now am old; yet have I not seen the righteous forsaken, nor his seed begging bread. He is ever merciful, and lendeth; and his seed is blessed." *(Ps. 37:25-26)*

David's son Solomon words on choosing the right wisdom

"The fear of the Lord is the beginning of wisdom: and the knowledge of the holy is understanding." *(Prov. 9:10)*

"Bow down thine ear, and hear the words of the wise, and apply thine heart unto my knowledge. [18] For it is a pleasant thing if thou keep them within thee; they shall withal be fitted in thy lips. [19] That thy trust may be in the Lord, I have made known to thee this day, even to thee. [20] Have not I written to thee excellent things in counsels and knowledge, [21] That I might make thee know the certainty of the words of truth; that thou mightest answer the words of truth to them that send unto thee."
(Prov. 22:17-21)

This is why Solomon was able to make such statements

"Behold, I have done according to thy words: lo, I have given thee a wise and an understanding heart; so that there was none like thee before thee, neither after thee shall any arise like unto thee. [13] And I have also given thee that which thou hast not asked, both riches, and honour: so that there shall not be any among the kings like unto thee all thy days. [14] And if thou wilt walk in my ways, to keep my statutes and my commandments, as thy father David did walk, then I will lengthen thy days." *(1 Kgs. 3:12-14)*

"And God gave Solomon wisdom and understanding exceeding much, and largeness of heart, even as the sand that is on the sea shore."
(1 Kgs. 4:29)

THINGS MONEY CAN'T BUY

Now meditate a moment on God's divine wisdom manifested in Solomon.

"My son, if thou wilt receive my words, and hide my commandments with thee; [2] So that thou incline thine ear unto wisdom, and apply thine heart to understanding; [3] Yea, if thou criest after knowledge, and liftest up thy voice for understanding; [4] If thou seekest her as silver, and searchest for her as for hid treasures; [5] Then shalt thou understand the fear of the Lord, and find the knowledge of God. [6] For the Lord giveth wisdom: out of his mouth cometh knowledge and understanding. [7] He layeth up sound wisdom for the righteous: he is a buckler to them that walk uprightly. [8] He keepeth the paths of judgment, and preserveth the way of his saints. [9] Then shalt thou understand righteousness, and judgment, and equity; yea, every good path. [10] When wisdom entereth into thine heart, and knowledge is pleasant unto thy soul; [11] Discretion shall preserve thee, understanding shall keep thee: [12] To deliver thee from the way of the evil man, from the man that speaketh froward things; [13] Who leave the paths of uprightness, to walk in the ways of darkness; [14] Who rejoice to do evil, and delight in the frowardness of the wicked; [15] Whose ways are crooked, and they froward in their paths: [16] To deliver thee from the strange woman, even from the stranger which flattereth with her words; [17] Which forsaketh the guide of her youth, and forgetteth the covenant of her God. [18] For her house inclineth unto death, and her paths unto the dead. [19] None that go unto her return again, neither take they hold of the paths of life. [20] That thou mayest walk in the way of good men, and keep the paths of the righteous. [21] For the upright shall dwell in the land, and the perfect shall remain in it. [22] But the wicked shall be cut off from the earth, and the transgressors shall be rooted out of it." *(Prov. 2:1-22)*

Don't bow to devilish wisdom

"But if ye have bitter envying and strife in your hearts, glory not, and lie not against the truth. [15] This wisdom descendeth not from above, but is earthly, sensual, devilish. [16] For where envying and strife is, there is confusion and every evil work. [17] But the wisdom that is from above is first pure, then peaceable, gentle, and easy to be intreated, full of mercy and good fruits, without partiality, and without hypocrisy." *(James 3:14-17)*

WISDOM OF GOD

"For I would that ye knew what great conflict I have for you, and for them at Laodicea, and for as many as have not seen my face in the flesh; [2] That their hearts might be comforted, being knit together in love, and unto all riches of the full assurance of understanding, to the acknowledgement of the mystery of God, and of the Father, and of Christ; [3] In whom are hid all the treasures of wisdom and knowledge." *(Col. 2:1-3)*

"Let the word of Christ dwell in you richly in all wisdom; teaching and admonishing one another in psalms and hymns and spiritual songs, singing with grace in your hearts to the Lord." *(Col. 3:16)*

"But unto them which are called, both Jews and Greeks, Christ the power of God, and the wisdom of God. [25] Because the foolishness of God is wiser than men; and the weakness of God is stronger than men." *(1 Cor. 1:24-25)*

"But of him are ye in Christ Jesus, who of God is made unto us wisdom, and righteousness, and sanctification, and redemption." *(1 Cor. 1:30)*

God has made His Son Jesus wisdom for you.

See additional references of others who walked in the wisdom of God.

Moses. Ex. 4:12; Acts 7:22. As God used Moses' wisdom from man, after you submit to Him, He will also use things such as secular education and training to establish His ultimate will in your life.

(Joseph - Gen. 41:38-39)
(Daniel - Dan. 1:17,2:23)
(Paul - Acts 22:3)
(Stephen - Acts 6:5,10)

THINGS MONEY CAN'T BUY

Paul

"For I am not ashamed of the gospel of Christ: for it is the power of God unto salvation to every one that believeth; to the Jew first, and also to the Greek. [17] For therein is the righteousness of God revealed from faith to faith: as it is written, The just shall live by faith." *(Rom. 1:16-17)*

In the following words of Solomon, he makes it crystal clear that no amount of money or anything is valued enough to buy wisdom.

"Happy is the man that findeth wisdom, and the man that getteth understanding. [14] For the merchandise of it is better than the merchandise of silver, and the gain thereof than fine gold. [15] She is more precious than rubies: and all the things thou canst desire are not to be compared unto her." *(Prov. 3:14-15)*

"And thou, Ezra, after the wisdom of thy God, that is in thine hand, set magistrates and judges, which may judge all the people that are beyond the river, all such as know the laws of thy God; and teach ye them that know them not." *(Ezra 7:25)*

When God gives you wisdom, it is your duty as it was Ezra to teach others.

Money without the wisdom of God

"For wisdom is a defence, and money is a defence: but the excellency of knowledge is, that wisdom giveth life to them that have it." *(Eccl. 7:12)*

The wisdom of God is more valuable than money

"Receive my instruction, and not silver; and knowledge rather than choice gold. [11] For wisdom is better than rubies; and all the things that may be desired are not to be compared to it." *(Prov. 8:10-11)*

"How much better is it to get wisdom than gold! and to get understanding rather to be chosen than silver!" *(Prov. 16:16)*

Job's discourse on wisdom

"But where shall wisdom be found? and where is the place of understanding? [13] Man knoweth not the price thereof; neither is it found in the land of the living. [14] The depth saith, It is not in me: and the sea saith, It is not with me. [15] It cannot be gotten for gold, neither shall silver be weighed for the price thereof. [16] It cannot be valued with the gold of Ophir, with the precious onyx, or the sapphire. [17] The gold and the crystal cannot equal it: and the exchange of it shall not be for jewels of fine gold. [18] No mention shall be made of coral, or of pearls: for the price of wisdom is above rubies. [19] The topaz of Ethiopia shall not equal it, neither shall it be valued with pure gold. [20] Whence then cometh wisdom? and where is the place of understanding? [21] Seeing it is hid from the eyes of all living, and kept close from the fowls of the air. [22] Destruction and death say, We have heard the fame thereof with our ears. [23] God understandeth the way thereof, and he knoweth the place thereof." *(Job 28:12-23)*

Solomon's discourse on wisdom

"For God giveth to a man that is good in his sight wisdom, and knowledge, and joy: but to the sinner he giveth travail, to gather and to heap up, that he may give to him that is good before God. This also is vanity and vexation of spirit." *(Eccl. 2:26)*

The voice of wisdom

When you seek the wisdom of God, the blessings of God are given to you.

"Riches and honour are with me; yea, durable riches and righteousness. [19] My fruit is better than gold, yea, than fine gold; and my revenue than choice silver. [20] I lead in the way of righteousness, in the midst of the paths of judgment: [21] That I may cause those that love me to inherit substance; and I will fill their treasures." *(Prov. 8:18-21)*

CHAPTER 25

GLADNESS OF HEART

David's thanks to God for the gladness in His presence

"Glory and honour are in his presence; strength and gladness are in his place." *(1 Chr. 16:27)*

David knew who put gladness (joy) in his heart

"Thou hast put gladness in my heart, more than in the time that their corn and their wine increased." *(Ps. 4:7)*

"Thou hast turned for me my mourning into dancing: thou hast put off my sackcloth, and girded me with gladness." *(Ps. 30:11)*

   Whatever you are going through in life, always remember that God will anoint you with the spirit of gladness to walk in victory.

"Thou lovest righteousness, and hatest wickedness: therefore God, thy God, hath anointed thee with the oil of gladness above thy fellows." *(Ps. 45:7)*

Remember the children of Israel

"And he brought forth his people with joy, and his chosen with gladness." *(Ps. 105:43)* See additional reference. Ex. 12:40-51

"The hope of the righteous shall be gladness: but the expectation of the wicked shall perish." *(Prov. 10:28)*

"Every man also to whom God hath given riches and wealth, and hath given him power to eat thereof, and to take his portion, and to rejoice in his labour; this is the gift of God. [20] For he shall not much remember the days of his life; because God answereth him in the joy of his heart."
(Eccl. 5:19-20)

"For great is the Lord, and greatly to be praised: he also is to be feared above all gods. [26] For all the gods of the people are idols: but the Lord made the heavens. [27] Glory and honour are in his presence; strength and gladness are in his place." (1 Chr. 16:25-27)

"For the kingdom of God is not meat and drink; but righteousness, and peace, and joy in the Holy Ghost." (Rom. 14:17)

"And not only so, but we also joy in God through our Lord Jesus Christ, by whom we have now received the atonement." (Rom. 5:11)

"But the fruit of the Spirit is love, joy, peace, longsuffering, gentleness, goodness, faith." (Gal. 5:22)

"Whom having not seen, ye love; in whom, though now ye see him not, yet believing, ye rejoice with joy unspeakable and full of glory." (1 Pet. 1:8)

Continuous seeking God - brings continuous gladness

"Let all those that seek thee rejoice and be glad in thee: and let such as love thy salvation say continually, Let God be magnified." (Ps. 70:4)

The future joy of the children of Israel

"And the ransomed of the Lord shall return, and come to Zion with songs and everlasting joy upon their heads: they shall obtain joy and gladness, and sorrow and sighing shall flee away." (Is. 35:10)

CHAPTER 26

SAFETY (a protected dwelling place)

Real safety can only be found in the Saviour – Jesus Christ.

Weapons of the enemy will be formed against you, but none will prosper.

"No weapon that is formed against thee shall prosper; and every tongue that shall rise against thee in judgment thou shalt condemn. This is the heritage of the servants of the Lord, and their righteousness is of me, saith the Lord." *(Is. 54:17)*

God can't lie and God can't fail

"God is not a man, that he should lie; neither the son of man, that he should repent: hath he said, and shall he not do it? or hath he spoken, and shall he not make it good." *(Num. 23:19)* See additional reference.
Heb. 6:17-19

David knew where his place of protection was

"I will both lay me down in peace, and sleep: for thou, Lord, only makest me dwell in safety." *(Ps. 4:8)*

You don't have to be afraid of anything

"I sought the Lord, and he heard me, and delivered me from all my fears. [5] They looked unto him, and were lightened: and their faces were not ashamed. [6] This poor man cried, and the Lord heard him, and saved him out of all his troubles. [7] The angel of the Lord encampeth round about them that fear him, and delivereth them." *(Ps. 34:4-7)*

"For God hath not given us the spirit of fear; but of power, and of love, and of a sound mind." *(2 Tim. 3:7)*

1. Power. See references. Luke 24:49; Acts 1:8; Rom. 8:15; 1 Cor. 16:10; 1 Tim. 4:14.
2. Love. See references. Gal. 5:22-23; 1 Cor. 13:4.
3. Sound mind. See references. 1 Tim. 2:9;3:2; Gal. 5:22-23; Titus 2:4-12.

When you are in the safety of God, He will take care of all of your needs and desires.

"The Lord is my shepherd; I shall not want." *(Ps. 23:1)*

"O fear the Lord, ye his saints: for there is no want to them that fear him. [10] The young lions do lack, and suffer hunger: but they that seek the Lord shall not want any good thing." *(Ps. 34:9-10)*

"For the Lord God is a sun and shield: the Lord will give grace and glory: no good thing will he withhold from them that walk uprightly." *(Ps. 84:11)*

"Truth shall spring out of the earth; and righteousness shall look down from heaven. [12] Yea, the Lord shall give that which is good; and our land shall yield her increase. [13] Righteousness shall go before him; and shall set us in the way of his steps." *(Ps. 85:11-13)*

Conditions for God's safety

"But whoso hearkeneth unto me shall dwell safely, and shall be quiet from fear of evil." *(Prov. 1:33)*

"When a man's ways please the Lord, he maketh even his enemies to be at peace with him." *(Prov. 16:7)*

"If ye abide in me, and my words abide in you, ye shall ask what ye will, and it shall be done unto you." *(John 15:7)*

"So shall my word be that goeth forth out of my mouth: it shall not return unto me void, but it shall accomplish that which I please, and it shall prosper in the thing whereto I sent it." *(Is. 55:11)*

Not found in idols (false gods)

"To whom will ye liken me, and make me equal, and compare me, that we may be like? [6] They lavish gold out of the bag, and weigh silver in the balance, and hire a goldsmith; and he maketh it a god: they fall down, yea, they worship. [7] They bear him upon the shoulder, they carry him, and set him in his place, and he standeth; from his place shall he not remove: yea, one shall cry unto him, yet can he not answer, nor save him out of his trouble. [8] Remember this, and shew yourselves men: bring it again to mind, O ye transgressors. [9] Remember the former things of old: for I am God, and there is none else; I am God, and there is none like me, [10] Declaring the end from the beginning, and from ancient times the things that are not yet done, saying, My counsel shall stand, and I will do all my pleasure." *(Is. 46:5-10)*

"After these things the word of the Lord came unto Abram in a vision, saying, Fear not, Abram: I am thy shield, and thy exceeding great reward." *(Gen. 15:1)*

"Be strong and of a good courage, fear not, nor be afraid of them: for the Lord thy God, he it is that doth go with thee; he will not fail thee, nor forsake thee." *(Deut. 31:6)*

"The eternal God is thy refuge, and underneath are the everlasting arms: and he shall thrust out the enemy from before thee; and shall say, Destroy them." *(Deut. 33:27)*

"There shall not any man be able to stand before thee all the days of thy life: as I was with Moses, so I will be with thee: I will not fail thee, nor forsake thee." *(Josh. 1:5)*

"Then said David to the Philistine, Thou comest to me with a sword, and with a spear, and with a shield: but I come to thee in the name of the Lord of hosts, the God of the armies of Israel, whom thou hast defied. [50] So David prevailed over the Philistine with a sling and with a stone, and smote the Philistine, and slew him; but there was no sword in the hand of David." *(1 Sam. 17:45,50)*

David & his son Absalom

"In thee, O Lord, do I put my trust; let me never be ashamed: deliver me in thy righteousness. [2] Bow down thine ear to me; deliver me speedily: be thou my strong rock, for an house of defence to save me. [3] For thou art my rock and my fortress; therefore for thy name's sake lead me, and guide me. [4] Pull me out of the net that they have laid privily for me: for thou art my strength. [5] Into thine hand I commit my spirit: thou hast redeemed me, O Lord God of truth. [6] I have hated them that regard lying vanities: but I trust in the Lord. [7] I will be glad and rejoice in thy mercy: for thou hast considered my trouble; thou hast known my soul in adversities; [8] And hast not shut me up into the hand of the enemy: thou hast set my feet in a large room." *(Ps. 3:1-8)*

See additional references. Ps. 3:3; 4:8; 5:11,12; 9:10; 18:2;30,35; 23:4; 27:1-3; 28:7; 32:7; 33:20; 34:4,6,7; 37:3,17; 61:3; 55:16-19; 57:2, 59:9; 71:3; 76:1-3; 119:114,117; 142:5.

Obedience to God's word will always keep you safe

"The Lord shall preserve thy going out and thy coming in from this time forth, and even for evermore." *(Ps. 121:8)*

Don't even worry about your enemies

"For the oppression of the poor, for the sighing of the needy, now will I arise, saith the Lord; I will set him in safety from him that puffeth at him." *(Ps. 12:5)*

"And David abode in the wilderness in strong holds, and remained in a mountain in the wilderness of Ziph. And Saul sought him every day, but God delivered him not into his hand." *(1 Sam. 23:14,30)*

"The name of the Lord is a strong tower: the righteous runneth into it, and is safe." *(Prov. 18:10)* See additional references. Prov. 18:11; Is. 25:12 NIV

"Lay not wait, O wicked man, against the dwelling of the righteous; spoil not his resting place: [16] For a just man falleth seven times, and riseth up again: but the wicked shall fall into mischief." *(Prov. 24:15-16)*

"The fear of man bringeth a snare: but whoso putteth his trust in the Lord shall be safe." *(Prov. 29:25)*

"Thou wilt keep him in perfect peace, whose mind is stayed on thee: because he trusteth in thee. [4] Trust ye in the Lord for ever: for in the Lord Jehovah is everlasting strength." *(Is. 26:3-4)*

"Fear thou not; for I am with thee: be not dismayed; for I am thy God: I will strengthen thee; yea, I will help thee; yea, I will uphold thee with the right hand of my righteousness." *(Is. 41:10)*

"For the Lord God will help me; therefore shall I not be confounded: therefore have I set my face like a flint, and I know that I shall not be ashamed. [8] He is near that justifieth me; who will contend with me? let us stand together: who is mine adversary? let him come near to me. [9] Behold, the Lord God will help me; who is he that shall condemn me? lo, they all shall wax old as a garment; the moth shall eat them up." *(Is. 50:7-9)*

God places a hedge of protection around His children.

The word protection comes from the Hebrew word Suwk "Sook". It means fence.

"Then Satan answered the Lord, and said, Doth Job fear God for nought? [10] Hast not thou made an hedge about him, and about his house, and about all that he hath on every side? thou hast blessed the work of his hands, and his substance is increased in the land. [11] But put forth thine hand now, and touch all that he hath, and he will curse thee to thy face. [12] And the Lord said unto Satan, Behold, all that he hath is in thy power; only upon himself put not forth thine hand. So Satan went forth from the presence of the Lord." *(Job 1:9-12)*

God will even protect His money that He places in your trust. This means that it must always be in His heavenly bank account.

"Lay not up for yourselves treasures upon earth, where moth and rust doth corrupt, and where thieves break through and steal: [20] But lay up for yourselves treasures in heaven, where neither moth nor rust doth corrupt, and where thieves do not break through nor steal: [21] For where your treasure is, there will your heart be also." *(Matt. 6:19-21)*

"And I give unto them eternal life; and they shall never perish, neither shall any man pluck them out of my hand. [29] My Father, which gave them me, is greater than all; and no man is able to pluck them out of my Father's hand." *(John 10:28-29)*

"Who art thou that judgest another man's servant? to his own master he standeth or falleth. Yea, he shall be holden up: for God is able to make him stand." *(Rom. 14:4)*

THINGS MONEY CAN'T BUY

Remember: In God, you are more than conquerors

"And we know that all things work together for good to them that love God, to them who are the called according to his purpose. [29] For whom he did foreknow, he also did predestinate to be conformed to the image of his Son, that he might be the firstborn among many brethren. [30] Moreover whom he did predestinate, them he also called: and whom he called, them he also justified: and whom he justified, them he also glorified. [31] What shall we then say to these things? If God be for us, who can be against us? [32] He that spared not his own Son, but delivered him up for us all, how shall he not with him also freely give us all things? [33] Who shall lay any thing to the charge of God's elect? It is God that justifieth. [34] Who is he that condemneth? It is Christ that died, yea rather, that is risen again, who is even at the right hand of God, who also maketh intercession for us. [35] Who shall separate us from the love of Christ? shall tribulation, or distress, or persecution, or famine, or nakedness, or peril, or sword? [36] As it is written, For thy sake we are killed all the day long; we are accounted as sheep for the slaughter. [37] Nay, in all these things we are more than conquerors through him that loved us. [38] For I am persuaded, that neither death, nor life, nor angels, nor principalities, nor powers, nor things present, nor things to come, [39] Nor height, nor depth, nor any other creature, shall be able to separate us from the love of God, which is in Christ Jesus our Lord." *(Rom. 8:28-39)*

"And he said unto me, My grace is sufficient for thee: for my strength is made perfect in weakness. Most gladly therefore will I rather glory in my infirmities, that the power of Christ may rest upon me." *(2 Cor. 12:9)*

Future destruction for the non-believer

"For when they shall say, Peace and safety; then sudden destruction cometh upon them, as travail upon a woman with child; and they shall not escape." *(1 Thess. 5:3)*

The assurance of safety for every child of God
"My sheep hear my voice, and I know them, and they follow me: [28] And I give unto them eternal life; and they shall never perish, neither shall any man pluck them out of my hand. [29] My Father, which gave them me, is greater than all; and no man is able to pluck them out of my Father's hand." *(John 10:27-29)*

Are you and your family in the ark of safety? If not, you should read the story of Noah. Genesis chapters six, seven and eight.

My prayer is that you will write the words of David from the book of Psalms chapter 91 on the tables of your heart. This is the secret of abiding in the ark of safety.

"He that dwelleth in the secret place of the most High shall abide under the shadow of the Almighty. [2] I will say of the Lord, He is my refuge and my fortress: my God; in him will I trust. [3] Surely he shall deliver thee from the snare of the fowler, and from the noisome pestilence. [4] He shall cover thee with his feathers, and under his wings shalt thou trust: his truth shall be thy shield and buckler. [5] Thou shalt not be afraid for the terror by night; nor for the arrow that flieth by day; [6] Nor for the pestilence that walketh in darkness; nor for the destruction that wasteth at noonday. [7] A thousand shall fall at thy side, and ten thousand at thy right hand; but it shall not come nigh thee. [8] Only with thine eyes shalt thou behold and see the reward of the wicked. [9] Because thou hast made the Lord, which is my refuge, even the most High, thy habitation; [10] There shall no evil befall thee, neither shall any plague come nigh thy dwelling. [11] For he shall give his angels charge over thee, to keep thee in all thy ways. [12] They shall bear thee up in their hands, lest thou dash thy foot against a stone. [13] Thou shalt tread upon the lion and adder: the young lion and the dragon shalt thou trample under feet. [14] Because he hath set his love upon me, therefore will I deliver him: I will set him on high, because he hath known my name. [15] He shall call upon me, and I will answer him: I will be with him in trouble; I will deliver him, and honour him. [16] With long life will I satisfy him, and shew him my salvation."

Future safety of all saints

"Him that overcometh will I make a pillar in the temple of my God, and he shall go no more out: and I will write upon him the name of my God, and the name of the city of my God, which is new Jerusalem, which cometh down out of heaven from my God: and I will write upon him my new name." (Rev. 3:12)

CHAPTER 27

PURIFICATION AFTER DEATH

(Also known as purgatory)

This belief is generally one in which many believe that after physical death, one can continue to experience the necessary cleansing in order to be found in the state of true holiness, when judged by God. That God in this after death state of continued suffering and pain will cleanse any and all sin that was present in that individual's life. This additional work will however, depend on the prayers and actions of those living. See Eph. 2:8-9; Titus 3:5

The word of God spoken by the prophet Ezekiel. He cried out against any such false doctrines.

"Behold, all souls are mine; as the soul of the father, so also the soul of the son is mine: the soul that sinneth, it shall die. [19] Yet say ye, Why? doth not the son bear the iniquity of the father? When the son hath done that which is lawful and right, and hath kept all my statutes, and hath done them, he shall surely live. [20] The soul that sinneth, it shall die. The son shall not bear the iniquity of the father, neither shall the father bear the iniquity of the son: the righteousness of the righteous shall be upon him, and the wickedness of the wicked shall be upon him. [21] But if the wicked will turn from all his sins that he hath committed, and keep all my statutes, and do that which is lawful and right, he shall surely live, he shall not die. [22] All his transgressions that he hath committed, they shall not be mentioned unto him: in his righteousness that he hath done he shall live. [23] Have I any pleasure at all that the wicked should die? saith the Lord God: and not that he should return from his ways, and live? [24] But when the righteous turneth away from his righteousness, and committeth iniquity, and doeth according to all the abominations that the wicked man doeth, shall he live? All his righteousness that he hath done shall not be mentioned: in his trespass that he hath trespassed, and in his sin that he hath sinned, in them shall he die. [25] Yet ye say, The way of the Lord is not equal. Hear now, O house of Israel; Is not my way equal? are not your ways unequal? [26] When a righteous man turneth away from his righteousness, and committeth iniquity, and dieth in them; for his iniquity that he hath done shall he die. [27] Again, when the wicked man turneth away from his wickedness that he hath committed, and doeth that which is lawful and right, he shall save his soul alive. [28] Because he considereth, and turneth away from all his transgressions that he hath committed, he shall surely live, he shall not die. [29] Yet saith the house of Israel, The way of the Lord is not equal. O house of Israel, are not my ways equal? are not your ways unequal? [30] Therefore I will judge you, O house of Israel, every one according to his ways, saith the Lord God. Repent, and turn yourselves from all your transgressions; so iniquity shall not be your ruin. [31] Cast away from you all your transgressions, whereby ye have transgressed; and make you a new heart and a new spirit: for why will ye die, O house of Israel? [32] For I have no pleasure in the death of him that dieth, saith the Lord God: wherefore turn yourselves, and live ye." *(Ezek. 18:4,19-32)*

The living blood of Christ can cleanse you from all sin. The blood of Jesus will never lose its power. See also. Mark 2:10; James 5:14-16

Peter understood the power of the blood

"Forasmuch as ye know that ye were not redeemed with corruptible things, as silver and gold, from your vain conversation received by tradition from your fathers; [19] But with the precious blood of Christ, as of a lamb without blemish and without spot: [20] Who verily was foreordained before the foundation of the world, but was manifest in these last times for you, [21] Who by him do believe in God, that raised him up from the dead, and gave him glory; that your faith and hope might be in God. [22] Seeing ye have purified your souls in obeying the truth through the Spirit unto unfeigned love of the brethren, see that ye love one another with a pure heart fervently: [23] Being born again, not of corruptible seed, but of incorruptible, by the word of God, which liveth and abideth for ever. [24] For all flesh is as grass, and all the glory of man as the flower of grass. The grass withereth, and the flower thereof falleth away: [25] But the word of the Lord endureth for ever. And this is the word which by the gospel is preached unto you." *(1 Pet. 1:18-25)*

You are commanded not to pray - intercede to the dead - or do anything to profane the name of God (Deut. 18:9-12; 1 Chr. 10:13-14; Is. 8:19-20).

This type of person is known as a necromancer. It is one who communicates with or interrogates the dead.

See 1 Samuel chapter twenty eight.

"Ye are the children of the Lord your God: ye shall not cut yourselves, nor make any baldness between your eyes for the dead." *(Deut. 14:1)*

"And they cried aloud, and cut themselves after their manner with knives and lancets, till the blood gushed out upon them." *(1 Kgs. 18:28)*

"Ye shall not make any cuttings in your flesh for the dead, nor print any marks upon you: I am the Lord." *(Lev. 19:28)*

"Neither shall men tear themselves for them in mourning, to comfort them for the dead; neither shall men give them the cup of consolation to drink for their father or for their mother." *(Jer. 16:7)*

"Weep ye not for the dead, neither bemoan him: but weep sore for him that goeth away: for he shall return no more, nor see his native country." *(Jer. 22:10)*

"Forbear to cry, make no mourning for the dead, bind the tire of thine head upon thee, and put on thy shoes upon thy feet, and cover not thy lips, and eat not the bread of men." *(Ezek. 24:17)*

You are not to offer any sacrifices of any kind to the dead

"I have not eaten thereof in my mourning, neither have I taken away ought thereof for any unclean use, nor given ought thereof for the dead: but I have hearkened to the voice of the Lord my God, and have done according to all that thou hast commanded me." *(Deut. 26:14)*

"They joined themselves also unto Baal-peor, and ate the sacrifices of the dead." *(Ps. 106:28)*

You will be judged at the end state of your walk

"And ye shall be hated of all men for my name's sake: but he that shall endure unto the end, the same shall be saved." *(Mark 13:13)*

"And he that overcometh, and keepeth my works unto the end, to him will I give power over the nations." *(Rev. 2:26)*

"And as it is appointed unto men once to die, but after this the judgment." *(Heb. 9:27)*

"Abstain from all appearance of evil. [23] And the very God of peace sanctify you wholly; and I pray God your whole spirit and soul and body be preserved blameless unto the coming of our Lord Jesus Christ. [24] Faithful is he that calleth you, who also will do it." *(1 Thess. 5:22-24)*

"He that is unjust, let him be unjust still: and he which is filthy, let him be filthy still: and he that is righteous, let him be righteous still: and he that is holy, let him be holy still. [14] Blessed are they that do his commandments, that they may have right to the tree of life, and may enter in through the gates into the city." *(Rev. 22:11,14)*

This position is saying that the work of Christ on the cross was not finished.

The following scriptures teach us that Jesus reversed the curse on man on earth.

"I have glorified thee on the earth: I have finished the work which thou gavest me to do. [19] And for their sakes I sanctify myself, that they also might be sanctified through the truth." *(John 17:4,19)*

"When Jesus therefore had received the vinegar, he said, It is finished: and he bowed his head, and gave up the ghost." *(John 19:30)*

See additional references. Eph. 5:26; Titus 2:14; 1 John 1:7-9,3:5-10; Matt. 1:21; Rev. 1:5

The heavenly intercessory ministry of Jesus is still on-going – that you might be purified enough to be found holy at His return in this life.

"Who is he that condemneth? It is Christ that died, yea rather, that is risen again, who is even at the right hand of God, who also maketh intercession for us." *(Rom. 8:34)* (Then - Mark 2:10; Now - James 5:14-16; 1 John 1:9)

"For we which have believed do enter into rest, as he said, As I have sworn in my wrath, if they shall enter into my rest: although the works were finished from the foundation of the world. [14] Seeing then that we have a great high priest, that is passed into the heavens, Jesus the Son of God, let us hold fast our profession. [15] For we have not an high priest which cannot be touched with the feeling of our infirmities; but was in all points tempted like as we are, yet without sin. [16] Let us therefore come boldly unto the throne of grace, that we may obtain mercy, and find grace to help in time of need." *(Heb. 4:3,14-16)*

"Wherefore he is able also to save them to the uttermost that come unto God by him, seeing he ever liveth to make intercession for them."
(Heb. 7:25)

"Wherefore Jesus also, that he might sanctify the people with his own blood, suffered without the gate." *(Heb. 13:12)*

"For Christ also hath once suffered for sins, the just for the unjust, that he might bring us to God, being put to death in the flesh, but quickened by the Spirit." *(1 Pet. 3:18)*

Christ work was truly perfected

"Who being the brightness of his glory, and the express image of his person, and upholding all things by the word of his power, when he had by himself purged our sins, sat down on the right hand of the Majesty on high."
(Heb. 1:3)

"For it became him, for whom are all things, and by whom are all things, in bringing many sons unto glory, to make the captain of their salvation perfect through sufferings." *(Heb. 2:10)*

"Though he were a Son, yet learned he obedience by the things which he suffered; [9] And being made perfect, he became the author of eternal salvation unto all them that obey him; [10] Called of God an high priest after the order of Melchisedec. [11] Of whom we have many things to say, and hard to be uttered, seeing ye are dull of hearing." *(Heb. 5:8-11)*

"Neither by the blood of goats and calves, but by his own blood he entered in once into the holy place, having obtained eternal redemption for us. [13] For if the blood of bulls and of goats, and the ashes of an heifer sprinkling the unclean, sanctifieth to the purifying of the flesh: [14] How much more shall the blood of Christ, who through the eternal Spirit offered himself without spot to God, purge your conscience from dead works to serve the living God? [15] And for this cause he is the mediator of the new testament, that by means of death, for the redemption of the transgressions that were under the first testament, they which are called might receive the promise of eternal inheritance. [23] It was therefore necessary that the patterns of things in the heavens should be purified with these; but the heavenly things themselves with better sacrifices than these." *(Heb. 9:12-15,23)*

Jesus defeated the power of Satan and sin

"He that committeth sin is of the devil; for the devil sinneth from the beginning. For this purpose the Son of God was manifested, that he might destroy the works of the devil." *(1 John 3:8)*

"If others be partakers of this power over you, are not we rather? Nevertheless we have not used this power; but suffer all things, lest we should hinder the gospel of Christ." *(1 Cor. 9:12)*

"What? know ye not that your body is the temple of the Holy Ghost which is in you, which ye have of God, and ye are not your own? [20] For ye are bought with a price: therefore glorify God in your body, and in your spirit, which are God's." *(1 Cor. 6:19-20)*

"Knowing that he which raised up the Lord Jesus shall raise up us also by Jesus, and shall present us with you." *(2 Cor. 4:14)*

"That he might sanctify and cleanse it with the washing of water by the word, [27] That he might present it to himself a glorious church, not having spot, or wrinkle, or any such thing; but that it should be holy and without blemish." *(Eph. 5:26-27)*

"If we confess our sins, he is faithful and just to forgive us our sins, and to cleanse us from all unrighteousness." *(1 John 1:9)*

"And they sung a new song, saying, Thou art worthy to take the book, and to open the seals thereof: for thou wast slain, and hast redeemed us to God by thy blood out of every kindred, and tongue, and people, and nation." *(Rev. 5:9)*

God's warning of trying to change His word

"For I testify unto every man that heareth the words of the prophecy of this book, If any man shall add unto these things, God shall add unto him the plagues that are written in this book: [19] And if any man shall take away from the words of the book of this prophecy, God shall take away his part out of the book of life, and out of the holy city, and from the things which are written in this book." *(Rev. 22:18-19)*

The finished sacrifice

"But this man, after he had offered one sacrifice for sins for ever, sat down on the right hand of God; [13] From henceforth expecting till his enemies be made his footstool. [14] For by one offering he hath perfected for ever them that are sanctified." *(Heb. 10:12-14)*

After death - there is judgement and no second chance to be saved

"And as it is appointed unto men once to die, but after this the judgment." *(Heb. 9:27)*

See additional reference.   Rev. 20:4-15

PURIFICATION AFTER DEATH

Read the following story of a rich man and a poor man

"There was a certain rich man, which was clothed in purple and fine linen, and fared sumptuously every day: [20] And there was a certain beggar named Lazarus, which was laid at his gate, full of sores, [21] And desiring to be fed with the crumbs which fell from the rich man's table: moreover the dogs came and licked his sores. [22] And it came to pass, that the beggar died, and was carried by the angels into Abraham's bosom: the rich man also died, and was buried; [23] And in hell he lift up his eyes, being in torments, and seeth Abraham afar off, and Lazarus in his bosom. [24] And he cried and said, Father Abraham, have mercy on me, and send Lazarus, that he may dip the tip of his finger in water, and cool my tongue; for I am tormented in this flame. [25] But Abraham said, Son, remember that thou in thy lifetime receivedst thy good things, and likewise Lazarus evil things: but now he is comforted, and thou art tormented. [26] And beside all this, between us and you there is a great gulf fixed: so that they which would pass from hence to you cannot; neither can they pass to us, that would come from thence. [27] Then he said, I pray thee therefore, father, that thou wouldest send him to my father's house: [28] For I have five brethren; that he may testify unto them, lest they also come into this place of torment. [29] Abraham saith unto him, They have Moses and the prophets; let them hear them. [30] And he said, Nay, father Abraham: but if one went unto them from the dead, they will repent. [31] And he said unto him, If they hear not Moses and the prophets, neither will they be persuaded, though one rose from the dead." *(Luke 16:19-31)*

Remember, you can not buy your way out of hell. Hell has no exits. Only Jesus has the power - the keys of hell and of death (Rev. 1:18).

CHAPTER 28

A HOLY CALLING

Read the holy calling of the apostle Paul in Acts 26:14-18; Gal. 1:15-16.

Preachers.

Paul's charge to Timothy

"Be not thou therefore ashamed of the testimony of our Lord, nor of me his prisoner: but be thou partaker of the afflictions of the gospel according to the power of God; [9] Who hath saved us, and called us with an holy calling, not according to our works, but according to his own purpose and grace, which was given us in Christ Jesus before the world began."
(2 Tim. 1:8-9)

Paul's first letter to the Corinthians

"Let every man abide in the same calling wherein he was called."
(1 Cor. 7:20)

Man made priests (ministers) are not ordained of God. Visit the story of Jeroboam's idolatry practice of trying to imitate God.

He developed a birthplace of evilness.

False religions.

"Whereupon the king took counsel, and made two calves of gold, and said unto them, It is too much for you to go up to Jerusalem: behold thy gods, O Israel, which brought thee up out of the land of Egypt. [29] And he set the one in Bethel, and the other put he in Dan. [30] And this thing became a sin: for the people went to worship before the one, even unto Dan. [31] And he made an house of high places, and made priests of the lowest of the people, which were not of the sons of Levi.

[32] And Jeroboam ordained a feast in the eighth month, on the fifteenth day of the month, like unto the feast that is in Judah, and he offered upon the altar. So did he in Bethel, sacrificing unto the calves that he had made: and he placed in Bethel the priests of the high places which he had made. [33] So he offered upon the altar which he had made in Bethel the fifteenth day of the eighth month, even in the month which he had devised of his own heart; and ordained a feast unto the children of Israel: and he offered upon the altar, and burnt incense." *(1 Kgs. 12:28-33)*
See also the false prophets of Baal & Asherah. 1 Kgs. 18:19,26-29,40

Man-made ministers are a work of Satan

"Therefore it is no great thing if his ministers also be transformed as the ministers of righteousness; whose end shall be according to their works." *(2 Cor. 11:15)*

Prophets.

"Then the Lord said unto me, The prophets prophesy lies in my name: I sent them not, neither have I commanded them, neither spake unto them: they prophesy unto you a false vision and divination, and a thing of nought, and the deceit of their heart." *(Jer. 14:14)*

"How long shall this be in the heart of the prophets that prophesy lies? yea, they are prophets of the deceit of their own heart." *(Jer. 23:26)*

Prophetess.

"Likewise, thou son of man, set thy face against the daughters of thy people, which prophesy out of their own heart; and prophesy thou against them, [18] And say, Thus saith the Lord God; Woe to the women that sew pillows to all armholes, and make kerchiefs upon the head of every stature to hunt souls! Will ye hunt the souls of my people, and will ye save the souls alive that come unto you? [19] And will ye pollute me among my people for handfuls of barley and for pieces of bread, to slay the souls that should not die, and to save the souls alive that should not live, by your lying to my people that hear your lies? [20] Wherefore thus saith the Lord God; Behold, I am against your pillows, wherewith ye there hunt the souls to make them fly, and I will tear them from your arms, and will let the souls go, even the souls that ye hunt to make them fly.

[21] Your kerchiefs also will I tear, and deliver my people out of your hand, and they shall be no more in your hand to be hunted; and ye shall know that I am the Lord. [22] Because with lies ye have made the heart of the righteous sad, whom I have not made sad; and strengthened the hands of the wicked, that he should not return from his wicked way, by promising him life: [23] Therefore ye shall see no more vanity, nor divine divinations: for I will deliver my people out of your hand: and ye shall know that I am the Lord." *(Ezek. 13:17-23)*

God's warning to the angel of the church and false prophetess (Rev. 2:18-23).

God's warning to workers of iniquity

"And the beast was taken, and with him the false prophet that wrought miracles before him, with which he deceived them that had received the mark of the beast, and them that worshipped his image. These both were cast alive into a lake of fire burning with brimstone." *(Rev. 19:20)*

"And the devil that deceived them was cast into the lake of fire and brimstone, where the beast and the false prophet are, and shall be tormented day and night for ever and ever." *(Rev. 20:10)*

God is the one who does the calling, commissioning and sending.

Biblical examples:
(Moses Ex. 3:4,4:21,3:10,8:1)
(Disciples Matt. 4:18; John 15:16; Matt. 28:16)

When you are truly called of God as Paul was, you will know. This will give you the power to resist being bought. See Ps. 37:25

"But none of these things move me, neither count I my life dear unto myself, so that I might finish my course with joy, and the ministry, which I have received of the Lord Jesus, to testify the gospel of the grace of God." *(Acts 20:24)*

"And I thank Christ Jesus our Lord, who hath enabled me, for that he counted me faithful, putting me into the ministry." *(1 Tim. 1:12)*

A HOLY CALLING

Saints.

"Who hath saved us, and called us with an holy calling, not according to our works, but according to his own purpose and grace, which was given us in Christ Jesus before the world began." *(2 Tim 1:9)* See additional references. 1 Corinthian chapter twelve and Romans chapter twelve.

If God has called you either as a preacher of the gospel, or as a follower of Christ who does not operate in the five-fold ministry, be forever faithful to your calling. For those of you who know you are in a position of holy calling by which man placed you there, read Acts 17:24 and 2 Chr. 7:14.

If someone has tried to buy you a holy calling, it is out of the will of God. The money is simply not worth you losing your anointing, and possibly your soul.

Remember Judas Iscariot, the disciple who betrayed Jesus. He had a holy calling from God. However, he allowed money (30 pieces of silver) from the religious representatives to fund his personal position of power outside his true calling. He got out of the will of God and lost his soul.

The safest place for you - is in the will of God. God is your true source, everything else is merely a resource. Follow the God given advice of Peter, Paul and David.

"Humble yourselves therefore under the mighty hand of God, that he may exalt you in due time: [7] Casting all your care upon him; for he careth for you." *(1 Pet. 5:6-7)*

"I can do all things through Christ which strengtheneth me. But my God shall supply all your need according to his riches in glory by Christ Jesus." *(Phil. 4:13,19)*

"The Lord is my shepherd; I shall not want. [2] He maketh me to lie down in green pastures: he leadeth me beside the still waters. [3] He restoreth my soul: he leadeth me in the paths of righteousness for his name's sake. [4] Yea, though I walk through the valley of the shadow of death, I will fear no evil: for thou art with me; thy rod and thy staff they comfort me.

[5] Thou preparest a table before me in the presence of mine enemies: thou anointest my head with oil; my cup runneth over. [6] Surely goodness and mercy shall follow me all the days of my life: and I will dwell in the house of the Lord for ever." *(Ps. chapter 23)*

Remember the story of king Saul who violated the priestly office of Samuel in the offering up of sacrificial offerings before God. When Saul tried to operate in an office in which he was not called to, God immediately judged him.

"And he tarried seven days, according to the set time that Samuel had appointed: but Samuel came not to Gilgal; and the people were scattered from him. [9] And Saul said, Bring hither a burnt offering to me, and peace offerings. And he offered the burnt offering. [10] And it came to pass, that as soon as he had made an end of offering the burnt offering, behold, Samuel came; and Saul went out to meet him, that he might salute him. [11] And Samuel said, What hast thou done? And Saul said, Because I saw that the people were scattered from me, and that thou camest not within the days appointed, and that the Philistines gathered themselves together at Michmash; [12] Therefore said I, The Philistines will come down now upon me to Gilgal, and I have not made supplication unto the Lord: I forced myself therefore, and offered a burnt offering. [13] And Samuel said to Saul, Thou hast done foolishly: thou hast not kept the commandment of the Lord thy God, which he commanded thee: for now would the Lord have established thy kingdom upon Israel for ever. [14] But now thy kingdom shall not continue: the Lord hath sought him a man after his own heart, and the Lord hath commanded him to be captain over his people, because thou hast not kept that which the Lord commanded thee." *(1 Sam. 13:8-14)*

Examples of other holy callings of God

(Abraham - Gen. 12:1, Acts 7:2)
(Samuel - 1 Sam. 3:4-11)
(David - 1 Sam. 16:10-13)
(Jeremiah - Jer. 1:4-10)
(Barnabas & Saul - Acts 13:1-3)
(12 Disciples - Matt. 10:1; Mark 3:13; Luke 6:12-16)

CHAPTER 29

TRUE COMFORT

Let us look at the source of true comfort.

True consolation can only be found in the true and living God.

David said this of God comforting him

"I sought the Lord, and he heard me, and delivered me from all my fears." *(Ps. 34:4)*

"I, even I, am he that comforteth you: who art thou, that thou shouldest be afraid of a man that shall die, and of the son of man which shall be made as grass; [13] And forgettest the Lord thy maker, that hath stretched forth the heavens, and laid the foundations of the earth; and hast feared continually every day because of the fury of the oppressor, as if he were ready to destroy? and where is the fury of the oppressor." *(Is. 51:12-13)*

The prophet Isaiah prophesied of Jesus coming to comfort those that mourn.

"To proclaim the acceptable year of the Lord, and the day of vengeance of our God; to comfort all that mourn; [3] To appoint unto them that mourn in Zion, to give unto them beauty for ashes, the oil of joy for mourning, the garment of praise for the spirit of heaviness; that they might be called trees of righteousness, the planting of the Lord, that he might be glorified." *(Is. 61:2-3)*

TRUE COMFORT

The fulfillment of the prophecy

"And he came to Nazareth, where he had been brought up: and, as his custom was, he went into the synagogue on the sabbath day, and stood up for to read. [17] And there was delivered unto him the book of the prophet Esaias. And when he had opened the book, he found the place where it was written, [18] The Spirit of the Lord is upon me, because he hath anointed me to preach the gospel to the poor; he hath sent me to heal the brokenhearted, to preach deliverance to the captives, and recovering of sight to the blind, to set at liberty them that are bruised, [19] To preach the acceptable year of the Lord." *(Luke 4:16-19)*

The beginning of Paul's second letter to the Corinthians emphasized the fact of God being the God of comfort.

"Blessed be God, even the Father of our Lord Jesus Christ, the Father of mercies, and the God of all comfort; [4] Who comforteth us in all our tribulation, that we may be able to comfort them which are in any trouble, by the comfort wherewith we ourselves are comforted of God." *(2 Cor. 1:3-4)*

The comfort of God is manifested in various ways. Please note some of the following ways.

In the Father

"Let not your heart be troubled: ye believe in God, believe also in me. [2] In my Father's house are many mansions: if it were not so, I would have told you. I go to prepare a place for you. [3] And if I go and prepare a place for you, I will come again, and receive you unto myself; that where I am, there ye may be also." (*John 14:1-3*)

"But my God shall supply all your need according to his riches in glory by Christ Jesus. [20] Now unto God and our Father be glory for ever and ever. Amen." *(Phil. 4:19-20)*

In the Son

"And he that searcheth the hearts knoweth what is the mind of the Spirit, because he maketh intercession for the saints according to the will of God. [34] Who is he that condemneth? It is Christ that died, yea rather, that is risen again, who is even at the right hand of God, who also maketh intercession for us." *(Rom. 8:27,34)*

"But that ye may know that the Son of man hath power on earth to forgive sins, (then saith he to the sick of the palsy,) Arise, take up thy bed, and go unto thine house." *(Matt. 9:6)* See Matt. 11:28

"If we confess our sins, he is faithful and just to forgive us our sins, and to cleanse us from all unrighteousness." *(1 John 1:9)*

"And he said unto me, My grace is sufficient for thee: for my strength is made perfect in weakness. Most gladly therefore will I rather glory in my infirmities, that the power of Christ may rest upon me." *(2 Cor. 12:9)*

In the word of God

"For whatsoever things were written aforetime were written for our learning, that we through patience and comfort of the scriptures might have hope." *(Rom. 15:4)*

"But he that prophesieth speaketh unto men to edification, and exhortation, and comfort." *(1 Cor. 14:3)*

"Let, I pray thee, thy merciful kindness be for my comfort, according to thy word unto thy servant." *(Ps. 119:76)*

"Let my heart be sound in thy statutes; that I be not ashamed." *(Ps. 119:80)*

See additional references. 1 Thess. 4:18; Luke 24:44; 2 Tim. 2:15,3:15-16

TRUE COMFORT

In preaching & spiritual gifts

"But he that prophesieth speaketh unto men to edification, and exhortation, and comfort. [31] For ye may all prophesy one by one, that all may learn, and all may be comforted." *(1 Cor. 14:3,31)*

In the Holy Ghost

"Then had the churches rest throughout all Judaea and Galilee and Samaria, and were edified; and walking in the fear of the Lord, and in the comfort of the Holy Ghost, were multiplied." *(Acts 9:31)* The comforter (consoler).

See additional references. John 14:16,26, 15:26, 16:13

In yourself

When there is a relationship with God.

David knew this

"I remembered thy judgments of old, O Lord; and have comforted myself." *(Ps. 119:52)*

Job knew this

"If I say, I will forget my complaint, I will leave off my heaviness, and comfort myself." *(Job 9:27)*

In Love

"If there be therefore any consolation in Christ, if any comfort of love, if any fellowship of the Spirit, if any bowels and mercies, [2] Fulfil ye my joy, that ye be likeminded, having the same love, being of one accord, of one mind." *(Phil. 2:1-2)*

THINGS MONEY CAN'T BUY

Family of God

"Wherefore comfort yourselves together, and edify one another, even as also ye do." *(1 Thess. 5:11)* See also. 1 Chr. 7:22,19:2

Fellowship of the Spirit

The comfort of the children of God in the spiritual realm. When God reveals to you through His various ways of speaking to you about certain issues.

(Abraham's fear - Gen. 5:1)
(Moses' call - Ex. 3:2-10)
(Hezekiah's answered prayer - Is. 38:4-5)
(Joseph's concern - Matt. 1:20)
(Revival of the gentiles - Acts chapter 10)
(Calling and sending forth of
Paul and Barnabas by the Holy Spirit - Acts chapter 13)

Prayer and supplications

"Likewise the Spirit also helpeth our infirmities: for we know not what we should pray for as we ought: but the Spirit itself maketh intercession for us with groanings which cannot be uttered. [27] And he that searcheth the hearts knoweth what is the mind of the Spirit, because he maketh intercession for the saints according to the will of God." *(Rom. 8:26-27)*

Praise & worship

"Praise ye the Lord: for it is good to sing praises unto our God; for it is pleasant; and praise is comely." *(Ps. 147:1)*

"To appoint unto them that mourn in Zion, to give unto them beauty for ashes, the oil of joy for mourning, the garment of praise for the spirit of heaviness; that they might be called trees of righteousness, the planting of the Lord, that he might be glorified." *(Is. 61:3)*

"The Lord is my strength and my shield; my heart trusted in him, and I am helped: therefore my heart greatly rejoiceth; and with my song will I praise him." *(Ps. 28:7)*

"Why art thou cast down, O my soul? and why art thou disquieted within me? hope thou in God: for I shall yet praise him, who is the health of my countenance, and my God." *(Ps. 42:11)*

"My soul shall be satisfied as with marrow and fatness; and my mouth shall praise thee with joyful lips: [6] When I remember thee upon my bed, and meditate on thee in the night watches." *(Ps. 63:5-6)*

"O Lord, thou art my God; I will exalt thee, I will praise thy name; for thou hast done wonderful things; thy counsels of old are faithfulness and truth." *(Is. 25:1)* See also. Ps. 95:6-7; John 10:28-29

The future comfort of Zion

"For the Lord shall comfort Zion: he will comfort all her waste places; and he will make her wilderness like Eden, and her desert like the garden of the Lord; joy and gladness shall be found therein, thanksgiving, and the voice of melody." *(Is. 51:3,12)*

See additional references. Is. 2:2-4, 9:6-7, 35:1-10

All who live righteous have the assurance of God's comfort

"Hearken unto me, ye that know righteousness, the people in whose heart is my law; fear ye not the reproach of men, neither be ye afraid of their revilings." *(Is. 51:7)*

"Paul, a servant of Jesus Christ, called to be an apostle, separated unto the gospel of God, [2] (Which he had promised afore by his prophets in the holy scriptures,) [3] Concerning his Son Jesus Christ our Lord, which was made of the seed of David according to the flesh; [4] And declared to be the Son of God with power, according to the spirit of holiness, by the resurrection from the dead: [5] By whom we have received grace and apostleship, for obedience to the faith among all nations, for his name. [16] For I am not ashamed of the gospel of Christ: for it is the power of God unto salvation to every one that believeth; to the Jew first, and also to the Greek. [17] For therein is the righteousness of God revealed from faith to faith: as it is written, The just shall live by faith." *(Rom. 1:1-5,16,17)*

CHAPTER 30

RIGHTEOUSNESS

The word righteousness simply means the right standing and the doing of what is right in the eyes of God. If you are not living in God's righteousness, you do not have life. See references. Rom 8:10; 1 John 3:5-7

God's view of man's standing without His righteousness

"But we are all as an unclean thing, and all our righteousnesses are as filthy rags; and we all do fade as a leaf; and our iniquities, like the wind, have taken us away." *(Is. 64:6)*

"As it is written, There is none righteous, no, not one." *(Rom. 3:10)*

"For all have sinned, and come short of the glory of God." *(Rom. 3:23)*

See other references. Ps. 14:2-3,39:5; Eccl. 7:20; 1 Cor. 15:34; Phil. 3:9; Luke 18:9-14; Rom. 10:1-13

The righteousness of God is free to all who accepts it through His plan of redemption

"But now the righteousness of God without the law is manifested, being witnessed by the law and the prophets; [22] Even the righteousness of God which is by faith of Jesus Christ unto all and upon all them that believe: for there is no difference: [23] For all have sinned, and come short of the glory of God; [24] Being justified freely by his grace through the redemption that is in Christ Jesus: [25] Whom God hath set forth to be a propitiation through faith in his blood, to declare his righteousness for the remission of sins that are past, through the forbearance of God; [26] To declare, I say, at this time his righteousness: that he might be just, and the justifier of him which believeth in Jesus." *(Rom. 3:21-26)*

RIGHTEOUSNESS

God looks on the inner-man

"But the Lord said unto Samuel, Look not on his countenance, or on the height of his stature; because I have refused him: for the Lord seeth not as man seeth; for man looketh on the outward appearance, but the Lord looketh on the heart." *(1 Sam. 16:7)*   See also. Prov. 16:2

God is fully aware of self-righteousness

Jesus' words to the scribes and Pharisees

"Woe unto you, scribes and Pharisees, hypocrites! for ye are like unto whited sepulchres, which indeed appear beautiful outward, but are within full of dead men's bones, and of all uncleanness. [28] Even so ye also outwardly appear righteous unto men, but within ye are full of hypocrisy and iniquity." *(Matt. 23:27-28)*

Characteristics of a self-righteous person.

Wrong kind of zeal

"Brethren, my heart's desire and prayer to God for Israel is, that they might be saved. [2] For I bear them record that they have a zeal of God, but not according to knowledge." *(Rom. 10:1-2)*

Lack of understanding

"For they being ignorant of God's righteousness, and going about to establish their own righteousness, have not submitted themselves unto the righteousness of God." *(Rom. 10:3)*

THINGS MONEY CAN'T BUY

Trying to obtain it through the works of the law

"Whom God hath set forth to be a propitiation through faith in his blood, to declare his righteousness for the remission of sins that are past, through the forbearance of God; [26] To declare, I say, at this time his righteousness: that he might be just, and the justifier of him which believeth in Jesus. [27] Where is boasting then? It is excluded. By what law? of works? Nay: but by the law of faith. [28] Therefore we conclude that a man is justified by faith without the deeds of the law. [29] Is he the God of the Jews only? is he not also of the Gentiles? Yes, of the Gentiles also: [30] Seeing it is one God, which shall justify the circumcision by faith, and uncircumcision through faith. [31] Do we then make void the law through faith? God forbid: yea, we establish the law." (*Rom. 3:25-31*)   See also. Rom. 4:5

Pious outward appearance

"Having a form of godliness, but denying the power thereof: from such turn away." *(2 Tim. 3:5)*

Your salvation must go beyond your outward appearance.

"Whose adorning let it not be that outward adorning of plaiting the hair, and of wearing of gold, or of putting on of apparel." *(1 Pet. 3:3)*

To receive the righteousness of God

"The Lord hath made known his salvation: his righteousness hath he openly shewed in the sight of the heathen." *(Ps. 98:2)*

"If we confess our sins, he is faithful and just to forgive us our sins, and to cleanse us from all unrighteousness." *(1 John 1:9)*

"That if thou shalt confess with thy mouth the Lord Jesus, and shalt believe in thine heart that God hath raised him from the dead, thou shalt be saved." *(Rom. 10:9-10)*

RIGHTEOUSNESS

The word of God teaches you that the righteousness of God is continuously revealed through His word.

"For I am not ashamed of the gospel of Christ: for it is the power of God unto salvation to every one that believeth; to the Jew first, and also to the Greek. [17] For therein is the righteousness of God revealed from faith to faith: as it is written, The just shall live by faith." *(Rom. 1:16-17)*

Remember the source of righteousness

"Drop down, ye heavens, from above, and let the skies pour down righteousness: let the earth open, and let them bring forth salvation, and let righteousness spring up together; I the Lord have created it." *(Is. 45:8)*

"For he hath made him to be sin for us, who knew no sin; that we might be made the righteousness of God in him." *(2 Cor. 5:21)*

"And be found in him, not having mine own righteousness, which is of the law, but that which is through the faith of Christ, the righteousness which is of God by faith:" *(Phil. 3:9)*

Doing righteousness

"If ye know that he is righteous, ye know that every one that doeth righteousness is born of him." *(1 John 2:29)*

"Little children, let no man deceive you: he that doeth righteousness is righteous, even as he is righteous." *(1 John 3:7)*

See additional references. Rom. 10:3-4; Gal. 2:20-21

CHAPTER 31

GOD

There is only one true and living divine sovereign God. He is the living God in the Holy Bible. All other gods are false gods. Any god that can be controlled, can be bought. God (Jehovah) is the self-existent one (Ex. 3:14) - and the self-sufficient one (Gen. 22:14). He (God) takes no bribes (2 Chr. 19:7; Deut. 10:17 AMP; Job 8:3 AMP).

God does not need any money (Psalms 50:7-12), however, you need a harvest (1 King 17:8-24), natural and spiritual.

The apostle John understood the working of God. He realized that every-thing began and ends with God. He is the only one that is self-sufficient. He is the owner of everything already. There is a saying in the world - "every-one has his or her limit". This is absolutely true with man. However, this does not apply to God, nor His faithful followers.

"In the beginning was the Word, and the Word was with God, and the Word was God. [2] The same was in the beginning with God. [3] All things were made by him; and without him was not any thing made that was made. [4] In him was life; and the life was the light of men. [5] And the light shineth in darkness; and the darkness comprehended it not." *(John 1:1-5)*
See Proverbs chapter 8 for the call of wisdom.

"Wherefore thou art great, O Lord God: for there is none like thee, neither is there any God beside thee, according to all that we have heard with our ears." *(2 Sam. 7:22)*

"O Lord, there is none like thee, neither is there any God beside thee, according to all that we have heard with our ears." *(1 Chr. 17:20)*

"And Melchizedek king of Salem brought forth bread and wine: and he was the priest of the most high God. [19] And he blessed him, and said, Blessed be Abram of the most high God, possessor of heaven and earth: [20] And blessed be the most high God, which hath delivered thine enemies into thy hand. And he gave him tithes of all." *(Gen. 14:18-20)*

"Unto thee it was shewed, that thou mightest know that the Lord he is God; there is none else beside him." *(Deut. 4:35)*

"For by him were all things created, that are in heaven, and that are in earth, visible and invisible, whether they be thrones, or dominions, or principalities, or powers: all things were created by him, and for him."
(Col. 1:16)

Since God already owns everything in the heavens and earth, He can't be bought. Men are either good stewards or bad stewards of what belongs to God.

God is the owner of all things

"Thine, O Lord, is the greatness, and the power, and the glory, and the victory, and the majesty: for all that is in the heaven and in the earth is thine; thine is the kingdom, O Lord, and thou art exalted as head above all. [12] Both riches and honour come of thee, and thou reignest over all; and in thine hand is power and might; and in thine hand it is to make great, and to give strength unto all." *(1 Chr. 29:11-12)*

"Thou art worthy, O Lord, to receive glory and honour and power: for thou hast created all things, and for thy pleasure they are and were created." *(Rev. 4:11)*

"The earth is the Lord's, and the fulness thereof; the world, and they that dwell therein." *(Ps. 24:1)*

Additional references. 1 Chr. 29:13-16; Ps. 103:19; Rom. 14:7-9; 1 Cor. 6:19-20; Heb. 1:2; Ps. 47:2,8

The true perspective

"Thus saith the Lord, The heaven is my throne, and the earth is my footstool: where is the house that ye build unto me? and where is the place of my rest." *(Is. 66:1)*

"Nor by the earth; for it is his footstool: neither by Jerusalem; for it is the city of the great King." *(Matt. 5:35)*

THINGS MONEY CAN'T BUY

The heavens and earth belong to God

"The heavens are thine, the earth also is thine: as for the world and the fulness thereof, thou hast founded them." *(Ps. 89:11)*

"For the earth is the Lord's, and the fulness thereof." *(1 Cor. 10:26)*

See additional references. Ex. 9:29; Deut. 10:14; Acts 17:24; Rev. 11:15

The land belongs to God

"The land shall not be sold for ever: for the land is mine; for ye are strangers and sojourners with me." *(Lev. 25:23)*

The animals belong to God

"I will take no bullock out of thy house, nor he goats out of thy folds. [10] For every beast of the forest is mine, and the cattle upon a thousand hills. [11] I know all the fowls of the mountains: and the wild beasts of the field are mine." *(Ps. 50:9-11)*

You belong to God

"For ye are bought with a price: therefore glorify God in your body, and in your spirit, which are God's." *(1 Cor. 6:20)*

See also. Num. 16:22; Ps. 95:6,100:3; Prov. 22:2; Jer. 32:37; Ezek. 18:4; John 1:3; Job 10:8, 12:10, 33:4; 1 Cor. 6:19; 1 Cor. 7:23; 1 Pet. 1:18-23

"What? know ye not that your body is the temple of the Holy Ghost which is in you, which ye have of God, and ye are not your own." *(1 Cor. 6:19)*

The air you breathe belongs to God

"And the Lord God formed man of the dust of the ground, and breathed into his nostrils the breath of life; and man became a living soul." *(Gen. 2:7)*

"In whose hand is the soul of every living thing, and the breath of all mankind." *(Job 12:10)*

"The Spirit of God hath made me, and the breath of the Almighty hath given me life." *(Job 33:4)*   See also. Acts 17:25 Zech. 12:1

"Thus saith God the Lord, he that created the heavens, and stretched them out; he that spread forth the earth, and that which cometh out of it; he that giveth breath unto the people upon it, and spirit to them that walk therein." *(Is. 42:5)*

"For in him we live, and move, and have our being; as certain also of your own poets have said, For we are also his offspring." *(Acts 17:28)*

All the money belongs to God

"The silver is mine, and the gold is mine, saith the Lord of hosts." *(Hag. 2:8)*   See also. Lev. 27:30; Josh. 6:19; Joel 3:5; Mal. 3:8

See additional references. Gen. 2:11-12; Ps. 95:6,100:3(NIV); Ex. 9:29,33, 19:5; Job 41:11; Deut. 10:14; 1 Cor. 6:20, 7:23; Phil. 2:5, 4:8; Rom. 12:1-2; 1 Cor. 3:16-17, 4:7, 6:19-20; 1 Pet. 1:18-23; Acts 17:28; Heb. 1:3; Mic. 4:13; Zech. 14:14

All power belongs to God

"God hath spoken once; twice have I heard this; that power belongeth unto God." *(Ps. 62:11)*

"But Jesus beheld them, and said unto them, With men this is impossible; but with God all things are possible." *(Matt. 19:26)*

"He ruleth by his power for ever; his eyes behold the nations: let not the rebellious exalt themselves. Selah." *(Ps. 66:7)*

God's permissible will for evilness

"The Lord hath made all things for himself: yea, even the wicked for the day of evil." *(Prov. 16:4)*   See additional references. Rom. 1:18, 2:5

"That they shall drive thee from men, and thy dwelling shall be with the beasts of the field, and they shall make thee to eat grass as oxen, and they shall wet thee with the dew of heaven, and seven times shall pass over thee, till thou know that the most High ruleth in the kingdom of men, and giveth it to whomsoever he will." *(Dan. 4:25)*

"And all the inhabitants of the earth are reputed as nothing: and he doeth according to his will in the army of heaven, and among the inhabitants of the earth: and none can stay his hand, or say unto him, What doest thou?" *(Dan. 4:35)*

"Who will have all men to be saved, and to come unto the knowledge of the truth. [5] For there is one God, and one mediator between God and men, the man Christ Jesus." *(1 Tim. 2:4-5)*

"Which in his times he shall shew, who is the blessed and only Potentate, the King of kings, and Lord of lords." *(1 Tim. 6:15)*

"Thou art worthy, O Lord, to receive glory and honour and power: for thou hast created all things, and for thy pleasure they are and were created." *(Rev. 4:11)*

"And the seventh angel sounded; and there were great voices in heaven, saying, The kingdoms of this world are become the kingdoms of our Lord, and of his Christ; and he shall reign for ever and ever." *(Rev. 11:15)*

God is a holy God

"Who is like unto thee, O Lord, among the gods? who is like thee, glorious in holiness, fearful in praises, doing wonders?" *(Ex. 15:11)*

God has called you to holiness

"And that ye put on the new man, which after God is created in righteousness and true holiness." *(Eph. 4:24)*

"To the end he may stablish your hearts unblameable in holiness before God, even our Father, at the coming of our Lord Jesus Christ with all his saints." *(1 Thess. 3:13)*

"For God hath not called us unto uncleanness, but unto holiness." *(1 Thess. 4:7)*

"Notwithstanding she shall be saved in childbearing, if they continue in faith and charity and holiness with sobriety." *(1 Tim. 2:15)*

"Follow peace with all men, and holiness, without which no man shall see the Lord." *(Heb. 12:14)*

See additional reference. Romans chapter nine.

When God brings you out of Egypt (type of the world), don't respond like the children of Israel. They became very impatient and took the financial blessing (gold) and made them a false god that they could worship and control. In other words, they bought - made them a god. The true and living God can't be bought.

"And when the people saw that Moses delayed to come down out of the mount, the people gathered themselves together unto Aaron, and said unto him, Up, make us gods, which shall go before us; for as for this Moses, the man that brought us up out of the land of Egypt, we wot not what is become of him. [2] And Aaron said unto them, Break off the golden earrings, which are in the ears of your wives, of your sons, and of your daughters, and bring them unto me. [3] And all the people brake off the golden earrings which were in their ears, and brought them unto Aaron. [4] And he received them at their hand, and fashioned it with a graving tool, after he had made it a molten calf: and they said, These be thy gods, O Israel, which brought thee up out of the land of Egypt. [5] And when Aaron saw it, he built an altar before it; and Aaron made proclamation, and said, To morrow is a feast to the Lord." *(Ex. 32:1-5)*

See the book of Exodus chapter thirty two, for additional revelation.

THINGS MONEY CAN'T BUY

You need to know that there is no salvation outside of God

"Yet I am the Lord thy God from the land of Egypt, and thou shalt know no god but me: for there is no saviour beside me." *(Hos. 13:4)*

See additional references. Deut. 4:35,32:39; 1 Sam. 2:2; Is. 43:11, 44:6,44:8,45:5-6,45:21; Acts 4:10-12

There is only one road that leads to God

"Jesus saith unto him, I am the way, the truth, and the life: no man cometh unto the Father, but by me." *(John 14:6)*

"Enter ye in at the strait gate: for wide is the gate, and broad is the way, that leadeth to destruction, and many there be which go in thereat. Because strait is the gate, and narrow is the way, which leadeth unto life, and few there be that find it." *(Matt. 7:13-14)*

"Therefore if any man be in Christ, he is a new creature: old things are passed away; behold, all things are become new." *(2 Cor. 5:17)*

"As ye have therefore received Christ Jesus the Lord, so walk ye in him. And ye are complete in him, which is the head of all principality and power." *(Col. 2:6,10)*

An example of man trying to buy God

(Simon the sorcerer. Acts 8:9-24)

As many of the children of Israel bought them a god - all who serve (a god) - rather than (The God) - worship a false god.

See the idol worship. Ex. 32:1-6,20

CONCLUSION

Let me conclude this book on sharing with you the story of an individual who was blessed of God financially. One who became the wealthiest, wisest and most famous man throughout the earth, outside of Jesus. However, he ended up turning his heart from the God of Israel.

Solomon's beginning

David's charge.

"Now the days of David drew nigh that he should die; and he charged Solomon his son, saying, [2] I go the way of all the earth: be thou strong therefore, and shew thyself a man; [3] And keep the charge of the Lord thy God, to walk in his ways, to keep his statutes, and his commandments, and his judgments, and his testimonies, as it is written in the law of Moses, that thou mayest prosper in all that thou doest, and whithersoever thou turnest thyself." *(1 Kgs. 2:1-3)*

Solomon's humbleness. 1 Kgs. 3:7-9

He obeyed God.

"And Solomon loved the Lord, walking in the statutes of David his father: only he sacrificed and burnt incense in high places." *(1 Kgs. 3:3)*

God's promise to Solomon. 1 Kgs. 3:10-14

God fulfilled His promises to Solomon.

1. Enlarged heart.

   "And God gave Solomon wisdom and understanding exceeding much, and largeness of heart, even as the sand that is on the sea shore." *(1 Kgs. 4:29)*

203

2. Knowledge.

"And God gave Solomon wisdom and understanding exceeding much, and largeness of heart, even as the sand that is on the sea shore. [30] And Solomon's wisdom excelled the wisdom of all the children of the east country, and all the wisdom of Egypt. [31] For he was wiser than all men; than Ethan the Ezrahite, and Heman, and Chalcol, and Darda, the sons of Mahol: and his fame was in all nations round about. [32] And he spake three thousand proverbs: and his songs were a thousand and five. [33] And he spake of trees, from the cedar tree that is in Lebanon even unto the hyssop that springeth out of the wall: he spake also of beasts, and of fowl, and of creeping things, and of fishes. [34] And there came of all people to hear the wisdom of Solomon, from all kings of the earth, which had heard of his wisdom." *(1 Kgs. 4:29-34)*

3. Wisdom.
  (1 Kgs. 4:29-32) See above.

"And all the earth sought to Solomon, to hear his wisdom, which God had put in his heart." *(1 Kgs. 10:24)*

"And all the kings of the earth sought the presence of Solomon, to hear his wisdom, that God had put in his heart." *(2 Chr. 9:23)*

"Howbeit in the business of the ambassadors of the princes of Babylon, who sent unto him to enquire of the wonder that was done in the land, God left him, to try him, that he might know all that was in his heart." *(2 Chr. 32:31)* The world sought this man's wisdom.

4. Wealth.

"And I have also given thee that which thou hast not asked, both riches, and honour: so that there shall not be any among the kings like unto thee all thy days." *(1 Kgs. 3:13)*

"I got me servants and maidens, and had servants born in my house; also I had great possessions of great and small cattle above all that were in Jerusalem before me: [8] I gathered me also silver and gold, and the peculiar treasure of kings and of the provinces: I gat me men singers and women singers, and the delights of the sons of men, as musical instruments, and that of all sorts. [9] So I was great, and increased more than all that were before me in Jerusalem: also my wisdom remained with me." *(Eccl. 2:7-9)*

See additional references. 1 Kgs. 9:14,10:1-29

5. Honor & glory.
"And I have also given thee that which thou hast not asked, both riches, and honour: so that there shall not be any among the kings like unto thee all thy days." *(1 Kgs. 3:13)*

See additional references. 1 Kgs. 4:31,10:1-9

He became the richest and wisest man that ever lived outside of Jesus. See references. Matt. 12:42; John 13:16

"And I gave my heart to seek and search out by wisdom concerning all things that are done under heaven: this sore travail hath God given to the sons of man to be exercised therewith." *(Eccl. 1:13)*

As a new covenant believer, you have been given better promises than Solomon.

"And Jesus answering saith unto them, Have faith in God. [23] For verily I say unto you, That whosoever shall say unto this mountain, Be thou removed, and be thou cast into the sea; and shall not doubt in his heart, but shall believe that those things which he saith shall come to pass; he shall have whatsoever he saith. [24] Therefore I say unto you, What things soever ye desire, when ye pray, believe that ye receive them, and ye shall have them." *(Mark 11:22-24)*

CONCLUSION

Solomon's Ending

His downfall.

"But king Solomon loved many strange women, together with the daughter of Pharaoh, women of the Moabites, Ammonites, Edomites, Zidonians, and Hittites; [2] Of the nations concerning which the Lord said unto the children of Israel, Ye shall not go in to them, neither shall they come in unto you: for surely they will turn away your heart after their gods: Solomon clave unto these in love. [3] And he had seven hundred wives, princesses, and three hundred concubines: and his wives turned away his heart. [4] For it came to pass, when Solomon was old, that his wives turned away his heart after other gods: and his heart was not perfect with the Lord his God, as was the heart of David his father. [5] For Solomon went after Ashtoreth the goddess of the Zidonians, and after Milcom the abomination of the Ammonites. [6] And Solomon did evil in the sight of the Lord, and went not fully after the Lord, as did David his father. [7] Then did Solomon build an high place for Chemosh, the abomination of Moab, in the hill that is before Jerusalem, and for Molech, the abomination of the children of Ammon. [8] And likewise did he for all his strange wives, which burnt incense and sacrificed unto their gods. [9] And the Lord was angry with Solomon, because his heart was turned from the Lord God of Israel, which had appeared unto him twice, [10] And had commanded him concerning this thing, that he should not go after other gods: but he kept not that which the Lord commanded. [11] Wherefore the Lord said unto Solomon, Forasmuch as this is done of thee, and thou hast not kept my covenant and my statutes, which I have commanded thee, I will surely rend the kingdom from thee, and will give it to thy servant." *(1 Kgs 11:1-11)*

"And I gave my heart to seek and search out by wisdom concerning all things that are done under heaven: this sore travail hath God given to the sons of man to be exercised therewith." *(Eccl. 1:13)*

"And whatsoever mine eyes desired I kept not from them, I withheld not my heart from any joy; for my heart rejoiced in all my labour: and this was my portion of all my labour." *(Eccl. 2:10)*

Worldly women.

This was not approved by God.

"Neither shall he multiply wives to himself, that his heart turn not away: neither shall he greatly multiply to himself silver and gold." *(Deut. 17:17)*

"Lest thou make a covenant with the inhabitants of the land, and they go a whoring after their gods, and do sacrifice unto their gods, and one call thee, and thou eat of his sacrifice; [16] And thou take of their daughters unto thy sons, and their daughters go a whoring after their gods, and make thy sons go a whoring after their gods." *(Ex. 34:15-16)*

"And Solomon made affinity with Pharaoh king of Egypt, and took Pharaoh's daughter, and brought her into the city of David, until he had made an end of building his own house, and the house of the Lord, and the wall of Jerusalem round about." *(1 Kgs. 3:1)*

"But king Solomon loved many strange women, together with the daughter of Pharaoh, women of the Moabites, Ammonites, Edomites, Zidonians, and Hittites; [2] Of the nations concerning which the Lord said unto the children of Israel, Ye shall not go in to them, neither shall they come in unto you: for surely they will turn away your heart after their gods: Solomon clave unto these in love. [3] And he had seven hundred wives, princesses, and three hundred concubines: and his wives turned away his heart. [4] For it came to pass, when Solomon was old, that his wives turned away his heart after other gods: and his heart was not perfect with the Lord his God, as was the heart of David his father. [5] For Solomon went after Ashtoreth the goddess of the Zidonians, and after Milcom the abomination of the Ammonites. [6] And Solomon did evil in the sight of the Lord, and went not fully after the Lord, as did David his father. [7] Then did Solomon build an high place for Chemosh, the abomination of Moab, in the hill that is before Jerusalem, and for Molech, the abomination of the children of Ammon. [8] And likewise did he for all his strange wives, which burnt incense and sacrificed unto their gods. [9] And the Lord was angry with Solomon, because his heart was turned from the Lord God of Israel, which had appeared unto him twice." *(1 Kgs. 11:1-9)*

"Did not Solomon king of Israel sin by these things? yet among many nations was there no king like him, who was beloved of his God, and God made him king over all Israel: nevertheless even him did outlandish women cause to sin." *(Neh. 13:26)*

"Which yet my soul seeketh, but I find not: one man among a thousand have I found; but a woman among all those have I not found."
(Eccl. 7:28)

Wealth.

See the Splendor of Solomon. 1 Kgs. 10:14-29

Wayward heart.

"And whatsoever mine eyes desired I kept not from them, I withheld not my heart from any joy; for my heart rejoiced in all my labour: and this was my portion of all my labour." *(Eccl. 2:10)*

Worship of idol gods.

"And they shall answer, Because they forsook the Lord their God, who brought forth their fathers out of the land of Egypt, and have taken hold upon other gods, and have worshipped them, and served them: therefore hath the Lord brought upon them all this evil." *(1 Kgs. 9:9)*

"For Solomon went after Ashtoreth the goddess of the Zidonians, and after Milcom the abomination of the Ammonites." *(1 Kgs. 11:5)*

"Then did Solomon build an high place for Chemosh, the abomination of Moab, in the hill that is before Jerusalem, and for Molech, the abomination of the children of Ammon. [8] And likewise did he for all his strange wives, which burnt incense and sacrificed unto their gods." *(1 Kgs. 11:7-8)*

Worldly pleasures.

"And Solomon gathered together chariots and horsemen: and he had a thousand and four hundred chariots, and twelve thousand horsemen, whom he bestowed in the cities for chariots, and with the king at Jerusalem. [27] And the king made silver to be in Jerusalem as stones, and cedars made he to be as the sycomore trees that are in the vale, for abundance. [28] And Solomon had horses brought out of Egypt, and linen yarn: the king's merchants received the linen yarn at a price. [29] And a chariot came up and went out of Egypt for six hundred shekels of silver, and an horse for an hundred and fifty: and so for all the kings of the Hittites, and for the kings of Syria, did they bring them out by their means." *(1 Kgs. 10:26-29)*

"And I gave my heart to know wisdom, and to know madness and folly: I perceived that this also is vexation of spirit." *(Eccl. 1:17)*

"I said in mine heart, Go to now, I will prove thee with mirth, therefore enjoy pleasure: and, behold, this also is vanity." *(Eccl. 2:1)*

"I sought in mine heart to give myself unto wine, yet acquainting mine heart with wisdom; and to lay hold on folly, till I might see what was that good for the sons of men, which they should do under the heaven all the days of their life. [8] I gathered me also silver and gold, and the peculiar treasure of kings and of the provinces: I gat me men singers and women singers, and the delights of the sons of men, as musical instruments, and that of all sorts. [10] And whatsoever mine eyes desired I kept not from them, I withheld not my heart from any joy; for my heart rejoiced in all my labour: and this was my portion of all my labour. [11] Then I looked on all the works that my hands had wrought, and on the labour that I had laboured to do: and, behold, all was vanity and vexation of spirit, and there was no profit under the sun." *(Eccl. 2:3,8,10,11)*

See additional reference. 2 Chr. 9:13-27

CONCLUSION

Solomon's final view on life

"Except the Lord build the house, they labour in vain that build it: except the Lord keep the city, the watchman waketh but in vain." *(Ps. 127:1)*

"Be not righteous over much; neither make thyself over wise: why shouldest thou destroy thyself? [17] Be not over much wicked, neither be thou foolish: why shouldest thou die before thy time." *(Eccl. 7:16-17)*

"Let us hear the conclusion of the whole matter: Fear God, and keep his commandments: for this is the whole duty of man. [14] For God shall bring every work into judgment, with every secret thing, whether it be good, or whether it be evil." *(Eccl. 12:13-14)*

Paul's view

"Wherefore we labour, that, whether present or absent, we may be accepted of him. [10] For we must all appear before the judgment seat of Christ; that every one may receive the things done in his body, according to that he hath done, whether it be good or bad." *(2 Cor. 5:9-10)*

"For the grace of God that bringeth salvation hath appeared to all men, [12] Teaching us that, denying ungodliness and worldly lusts, we should live soberly, righteously, and godly, in this present world; [13] Looking for that blessed hope, and the glorious appearing of the great God and our Saviour Jesus Christ." *(Titus 2:11-13)*

"Follow peace with all men, and holiness, without which no man shall see the Lord: [15] Looking diligently lest any man fail of the grace of God; lest any root of bitterness springing up trouble you, and thereby many be defiled." *(Heb. 12:14-15)*

John's view

"And I saw a great white throne, and him that sat on it, from whose face the earth and the heaven fled away; and there was found no place for them. [12] And I saw the dead, small and great, stand before God; and the books were opened: and another book was opened, which is the book of life: and the dead were judged out of those things which were written in the books, according to their works. [13] And the sea gave up the dead which were in it; and death and hell delivered up the dead which were in them: and they were judged every man according to their works. [14] And death and hell were cast into the lake of fire. This is the second death. [15] And whosoever was not found written in the book of life was cast into the lake of fire." *(Rev. 20:11-15)*

Jesus' view

"For the Son of man shall come in the glory of his Father with his angels; and then he shall reward every man according to his works." *(Matt. 16:27)*

"For after all these things do the Gentiles seek: for your heavenly Father knoweth that ye have need of all these things. [33] But seek ye first the kingdom of God, and his righteousness; and all these things shall be added unto you." *(Matt. 6:32-33)*

"Teaching them to observe all things whatsoever I have commanded you: and, lo, I am with you alway, even unto the end of the world. Amen." *(Matt. 28:30)*

CONCLUSION

Don't forget the words of God to the children of Israel after fulfilling His promise to them.

"Therefore thou shalt keep the commandments of the Lord thy God, to walk in his ways, and to fear him. [7] For the Lord thy God bringeth thee into a good land, a land of brooks of water, of fountains and depths that spring out of valleys and hills; [8] A land of wheat, and barley, and vines, and fig trees, and pomegranates; a land of oil olive, and honey; [9] A land wherein thou shalt eat bread without scarceness, thou shalt not lack any thing in it; a land whose stones are iron, and out of whose hills thou mayest dig brass. [10] When thou hast eaten and art full, then thou shalt bless the Lord thy God for the good land which he hath given thee. [11] Beware that thou forget not the Lord thy God, in not keeping his commandments, and his judgments, and his statutes, which I command thee this day: [12] Lest when thou hast eaten and art full, and hast built goodly houses, and dwelt therein; [13] And when thy herds and thy flocks multiply, and thy silver and thy gold is multiplied, and all that thou hast is multiplied; [14] Then thine heart be lifted up, and thou forget the Lord thy God, which brought thee forth out of the land of Egypt, from the house of bondage; [15] Who led thee through that great and terrible wilderness, wherein were fiery serpents, and scorpions, and drought, where there was no water; who brought thee forth water out of the rock of flint; [16] Who fed thee in the wilderness with manna, which thy fathers knew not, that he might humble thee, and that he might prove thee, to do thee good at thy latter end; [17] And thou say in thine heart, My power and the might of mine hand hath gotten me this wealth. [18] But thou shalt remember the Lord thy God: for it is he that giveth thee power to get wealth, that he may establish his covenant which he sware unto thy fathers, as it is this day. [19] And it shall be, if thou do at all forget the Lord thy God, and walk after other gods, and serve them, and worship them, I testify against you this day that ye shall surely perish. [20] As the nations which the Lord destroyeth before your face, so shall ye perish; because ye would not be obedient unto the voice of the Lord your God." *(Deut. 8:6-20)*

Solomon's words on money without God

"If thou seest the oppression of the poor, and violent perverting of judgment and justice in a province, marvel not at the matter: for he that is higher than the highest regardeth; and there be higher than they. [9] Moreover the profit of the earth is for all: the king himself is served by the field. [10] He that loveth silver shall not be satisfied with silver; nor he that loveth abundance with increase: this is also vanity. [11] When goods increase, they are increased that eat them: and what good is there to the owners thereof, saving the beholding of them with their eyes? [12] The sleep of a labouring man is sweet, whether he eat little or much: but the abundance of the rich will not suffer him to sleep. [13] There is a sore evil which I have seen under the sun, namely, riches kept for the owners thereof to their hurt. [14] But those riches perish by evil travail: and he begetteth a son, and there is nothing in his hand. [15] As he came forth of his mother's womb, naked shall he return to go as he came, and shall take nothing of his labour, which he may carry away in his hand. [16] And this also is a sore evil, that in all points as he came, so shall he go: and what profit hath he that hath laboured for the wind? [17] All his days also he eateth in darkness, and he hath much sorrow and wrath with his sickness. [18] Behold that which I have seen: it is good and comely for one to eat and to drink, and to enjoy the good of all his labour that he taketh under the sun all the days of his life, which God giveth him: for it is his portion. [19] Every man also to whom God hath given riches and wealth, and hath given him power to eat thereof, and to take his portion, and to rejoice in his labour; this is the gift of God. [20] For he shall not much remember the days of his life; because God answereth him in the joy of his heart." *(Eccl. 5:8-20)*

CONCLUSION

God's warning for those that have been blessed with wealth and abuse the blessing

"Go to now, ye rich men, weep and howl for your miseries that shall come upon you. [2] Your riches are corrupted, and your garments are motheaten. [3] Your gold and silver is cankered; and the rust of them shall be a witness against you, and shall eat your flesh as it were fire. Ye have heaped treasure together for the last days. [4] Behold, the hire of the labourers who have reaped down your fields, which is of you kept back by fraud, crieth: and the cries of them which have reaped are entered into the ears of the Lord of sabaoth. [5] Ye have lived in pleasure on the earth, and been wanton; ye have nourished your hearts, as in a day of slaughter."
(James 5:1-5)

The apostle Paul's declaration of your completeness in Christ

"And ye are complete in him, which is the head of all principality and power." *(Col. 2:10)*

You will always be empty, dissatisfied or incomplete without Christ in your life, regardless of all the material - temporal things you might have. By the way, you can never truly possess things, however, material - temporal things can possess/controll you (Matt. 19:16-26).

To God be the Glory !

Other Books By Dr. Robert Mukes

The Need Meeter™

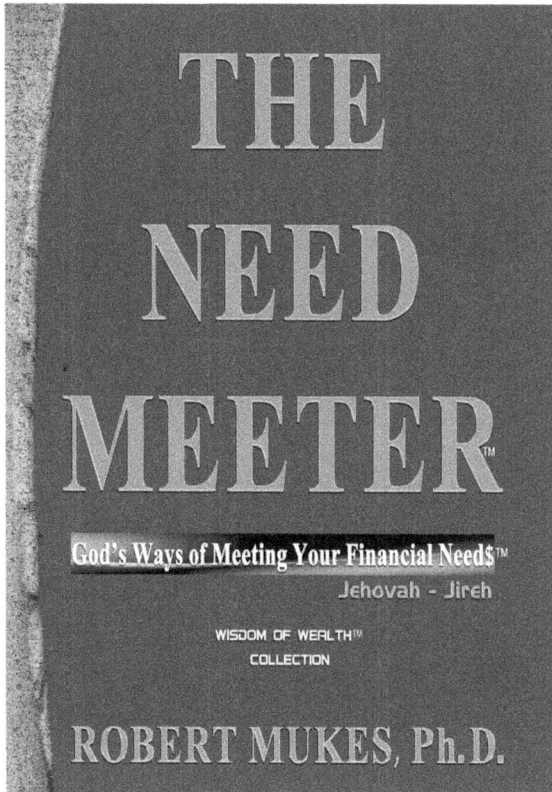

This book teaches you that God is your provider. You will learn your covenant responsibilities and God's eight (8) ways of meeting your financial needs and how to receive the desires of your heart. (74 Pages)

To order:

on the web at: www.amazon.com

What To Do With Money™

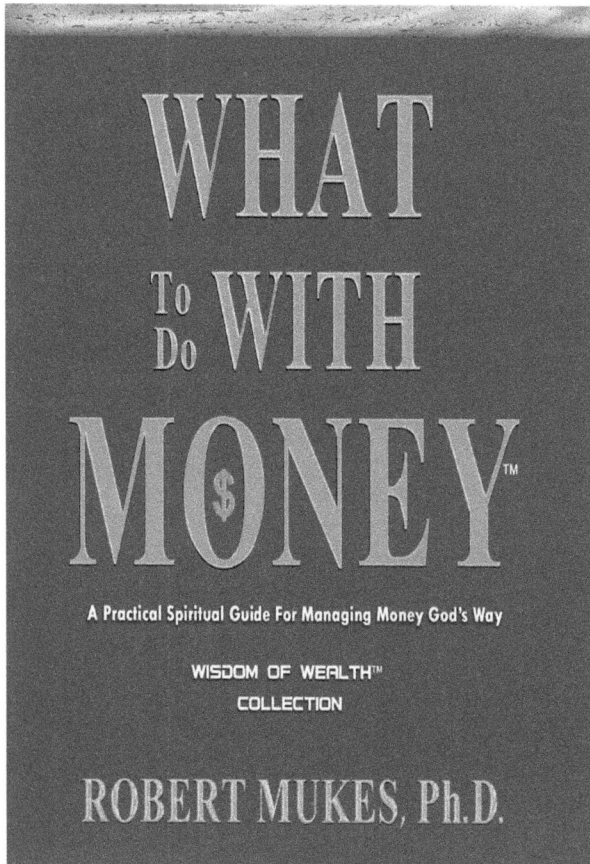

Would you like to learn God's principles for managing money faithfully ? In this book, Dr. Mukes teaches you the real truth about money. Are you prepared to give a true account of your stewardship ? This book teaches you how to get prepared.
(152 Pages)

To order:

on the web at: www.amazon.com

My latest book

I Know I'm Saved™

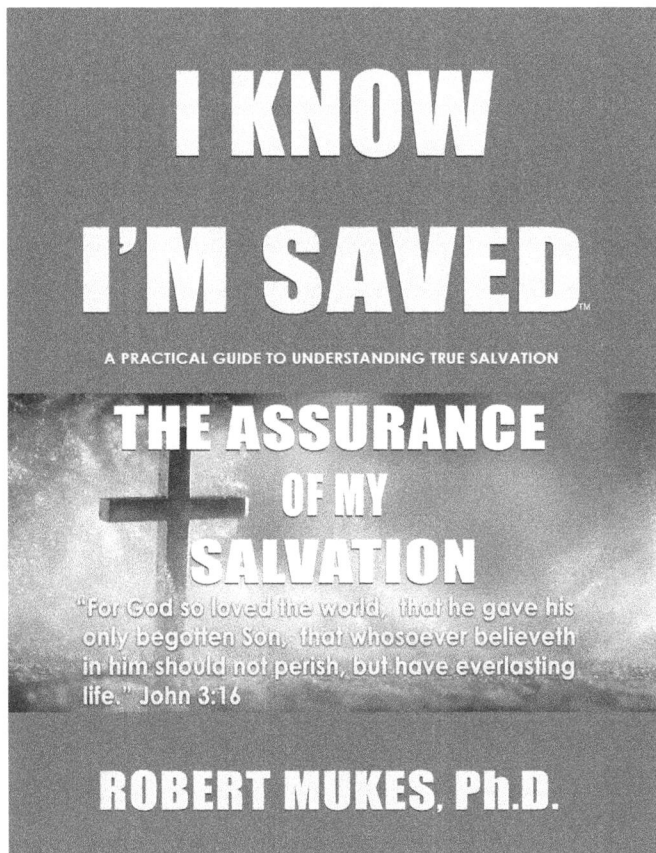

I KNOW I'M SAVED™

A PRACTICAL GUIDE TO UNDERSTANDING TRUE SALVATION

THE ASSURANCE OF MY SALVATION

"For God so loved the world, that he gave his only begotten Son, that whosoever believeth in him should not perish, but have everlasting life." John 3:16

ROBERT MUKES, Ph.D.

This book is a practical guide to understanding true salvation.
(85 Pages)

To order:

on the web at: www.amazon.com

www.ingramcontent.com/pod-product-compliance
Lightning Source LLC
Chambersburg PA
CBHW080500110426
42742CB00017B/2956